# Celebrating
# Reform 2007

## Doing Busine⸱ ⸱ase Studies

*16510)*

**IFC**
International
Finance
Corporation
World Bank Group

**THE WORLD BANK**

**USAID**
FROM THE AMERICAN PEOPLE

© 2007 The International Bank for Reconstruction and Development / The World Bank
1818 H Street NW
Washington, D.C. 20433
Telephone 202-473-1000
Internet www.worldbank.org
E-mail feedback@worldbank.org

2 3 4 5 09 08 07

This volume is a product of the staff of the World Bank Group. The findings, interpretations, and conclusions expressed in this volume do not necessarily reflect the views of the Executive Directors of The World Bank or the governments they represent. The World Bank Group does not guarantee the accuracy of the data included in this work. Publication was made possible by the United States Agency for International Development (USAID). The opinions expressed herein are those of author(s) and do not necessarily reflect the views of USAID or the United States Government.

**Rights and Permissions**

ISBN: 978-0-8213-7293-7
E-ISBN: 978-0-8213-7294-4
DOI: 10.1596/978-0-8213-7293-7

# Table of Contents

Preface     v

**Introduction**

**Celebrating reform**     1
SIMEON DJANKOV AND CARALEE MCLIESH

**Starting a business**
EL SALVADOR

**Starting a business (quickly) in El Salvador**     9
JAMES NEWTON, SYLVIA SOLF, AND ADRIANA VICENTINI

SERBIA

**How to double business entry in two years**     17
TOM JERSILD AND ZORAN SKOPLJAK

**Dealing with licenses**
GEORGIA

**Licensing 159 activities—not 909**     23
SVETLANA BAGAUDINOVA, DANA OMRAN AND UMAR SHAVUROV

**Employing workers**
MACEDONIA

**Employing Macedonia's youth**     31
ADAM LARSON, KIRIL MINOSKI, AND JANET MORRIS

**Registering property**
GEORGIA

**Need land administration reform? Start a revolution**     38
PENELOPE FIDAS AND JIM MCNICHOLAS

**Getting credit**
PANAMA

**Reforming the credit bureau law**     45
FREDERIC BUSTELO

**Protecting investors**
MEXICO

**Protecting investors from self-dealing**     51
MELISSA JOHNS AND JEAN MICHEL LOBET

**Paying taxes**
EGYPT

**Adding a million taxpayers**     60
RITA RAMALHO

**Trading across borders**
PAKISTAN

**Speeding up trade**     67
ALLEN DENNIS

**Enforcing contracts**
NIGERIA

**Repairing a car with the engine running**     73
SABINE HERTVELDT

**Closing a business**
SERBIA

**Faster, more orderly exit**     81
JUSTIN YAP

Acknowledgments     88

# Preface

Reforming business regulation takes leadership—more than many other reforms. Committed leaders provide vision, energy and direction to improving business climates, often in the face of daunting challenges.

The U.S. Agency for International Development and the World Bank Group are fortunate to work with many leaders around the world, some of whom are recognized in the accompanying case studies of reform. It has been a privilege to support their efforts and to see their results. We have also been pleased to partner together in many areas of this work, from pioneering "Investor Roadmaps" or "Administrative Barriers Analysis" together in Ghana in the mid-1990s, to collaborating in introducing the *Doing Business* project to sub-national governments and on the attached case studies.

We hope that the case studies will inspire others to reform business regulations. They feature successful reforms in the 10 areas covered in the *Doing Business* report. The case studies span the globe—from Serbia to El Salvador, from Egypt to Nigeria—and provide lessons on what it takes to succeed. It is through such efforts that governments can encourage businesses to invest, grow and create the jobs that lift people out of poverty.

Stephen J. Hadley
DIRECTOR
OFFICE OF ECONOMIC GROWTH
U.S. AGENCY
FOR INTERNATIONAL
DEVELOPMENT

Michael Klein
VICE PRESIDENT
FINANCIAL AND PRIVATE SECTOR DEVELOPMENT
WORLD BANK GROUP

# Celebrating reform

Simeon Djankov and Caralee McLiesh

Name your favorite dentist. Don't have one? That's because no one likes going to the dentist. Sometimes he gives you unpleasant news. Sometimes it hurts. Once you are healthy you stay as far away for as long as possible.

Reformers are like dentists. Necessary, but generally disliked. Their job is to cure the economy and create jobs. Very often this involves unpleasant news and it hurts, initially. In fact, reformers are even worse off than dentists: they are disliked even by their own kind. When a reformist minister says commercial disputes need to be resolved faster in the courts, the justice minister accuses him of ignorance. Or arrogance. Or both. When a reformist minister says labor regulations are too rigid and leave many people stranded in the informal economy, the labor minister accuses him of ignorance. Or arrogance. Or both.

In prosperous times, reformers are told not to rock the boat. In crisis times, they get the blame for not reforming sooner and averting the crisis. Some pursue reforms while receiving personal threats and threats to their families. It is hard to be a reformer.

Here are 3 ways to change that. First, document successful reforms and the challenges that had to be overcome along the way. This helps future reformers and highlights the contributions of past ones. Second, create a prize to recognize reformers. Movies have the Oscars, science has the Nobels, and sports have the Olympics. Reformers can have awards too. Finally, encourage reformers to write up their often dramatic stories. Imagine if these were turned into movies. It would only take a few films starring Jude Law, Angelina Jolie and George Clooney to make reformers more popular.

*Doing Business* develops the first idea, by presenting 11 case studies of recent reforms. These span the globe—from Serbia to El Salvador, from Egypt to Nigeria—and show what it takes to succeed. The case studies show several patterns. Reforms usually happen when new governments take office. They often follow crises. Reformers don't have time for concepts like "getting the right sequencing" and "finding the binding constraint." Reformers are helped by active media and information campaigns. And reforms may benefit from tapping development experts, outside expertise (be it from ISO9000 inspectors or Microsoft's software engineers) and lessons from other countries.

We also take on the second idea, by organizing the first annual awards for outstanding reformers (details available at www.reformersclub.org). The third idea is waiting for its champion.

## Reforms are on the rise

Reforms to make it easier for businesses to operate are on the rise. In 2005-06, 213 reforms took place in 112 countries. This compares with 185 reforms in 99 countries in 2004-05. And 89 reforms in 58 countries in 2003-04.

Four reasons explain the upswing. First, the collapse of socialism and the entry of Eastern Europe and the former Soviet Union in the world economy. Over the last decade, this region has led in reforms (figure 1). This is not surprising: the environment for doing business in the private sector was difficult so a lot had to be changed.

Second, the increase in global and regional competition. Regional agreements such as the US free trade agreements with Central American countries and accession of Eastern European countries into the European Union (EU) have generated huge reform momentum. Also, China has become everyone's competitor. In 2005-2006, 4 of the top-10 reformers have reformed to enter regional agreements: Croatia, Guatemala, Peru and Romania. China was a top reformer too (table 1). Countries are competing for investment, enterprises, and the jobs that come with them—and as a result it is getting easier to do business around the world.

Third, a new focus on reducing corruption. Many reforms to business regulation are made not to increase efficiency but to cut the corrupt practices of government officials. This is illustrated most vividly by Georgia, the top reformer in *Doing Business 2007* and also the country achieving the biggest drop in corruption in all of Europe—in 2002 37% of businesses said that they frequently paid bribes compared with only 8% in 2005.

FIGURE 1
**The pace of reform is strong in most regions outside of Asia**

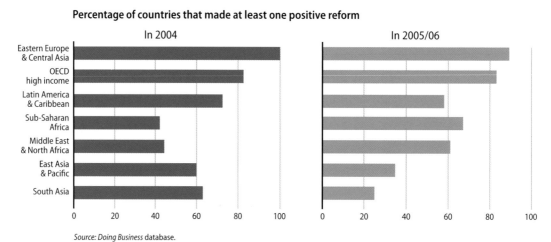

Percentage of countries that made at least one positive reform

*Source: Doing Business database.*

TABLE 1
**The top 10 reformers in 2005/06**

| Economy | Starting a business | Dealing with licenses | Employing workers | Registering property | Getting credit | Protecting investors | Paying taxes | Trading across borders | Enforcing contracts | Closing a business |
|---|---|---|---|---|---|---|---|---|---|---|
| Georgia | ✓ | ✓ | ✓ | | ✓ | | | ✓ | ✓ | |
| Romania | | ✓ | ✓ | | ✓ | ✓ | | ✓ | | ✓ |
| Mexico | ✓ | | | | | ✓ | ✓ | | | |
| China | ✓ | | | | ✓ | ✓ | | ✓ | | |
| Peru | ✓ | | | | ✓ | ✓ | | | ✓ | ✗ |
| France | | ✓ | | | ✓ | | | ✓ | ✓ | ✓ |
| Croatia | ✓ | | | ✓ | | | | | ✓ | |
| Guatemala | ✓ | ✓ | | ✓ | | | | | | |
| Ghana | | | | ✓ | | | ✓ | ✓ | | |
| Tanzania | ✓ | | | ✓ | | ✓ | | ✓ | | |

*Note:* Economies are ranked on the number and impact of reforms. First, *Doing Business* selects the economies that reformed in 3 or more of the *Doing Business* topics. Second, it ranks these economies on the increase in rank in the ease of doing business from the previous year. The larger the improvement, the higher the ranking as a reformer. "X" indicates a negative reform.
*Source: Doing Business* database.

Finally, what gets measured gets done. New indicators on business regulations in *Doing Business*—and from other sources—allow countries to identify bottlenecks and compare their performance with competitors. This inspires competition—no one likes looking worse than their neighbors. In 2000, EU countries agreed to track the time and cost to start a business. Since then, every EU country has made startup easier. The effect is even stronger when measurement is linked to financial incentives. When the United States' Millennium Challenge Account (MCA) made eligibility for funding dependent on the ease of business startup, countries from Burkina Faso to El Salvador to Georgia to Malawi started reforms. Indonesian Finance Minister Sri Mulyani Indrawati argues that the real impact of the MCA is its "good housekeeping seal of approval," which sends a powerful signal to investors. "It's not about the money. It's about the recognition that we're doing the right thing."

## How reforms are done

The existing manuals on reforms offer a simple recipe: take a strong reform champion, mix in highly-qualified technical staff, throw in valuable advice from development experts, stir it just the right amount of time, and serve while still hot. The problem is that reformers often miss some ingredients and the results can be a bit lumpy. Here are some ideas on substitutes.

A lot of reforms are sparked by crisis. But there's no need to wait for one to get change—crises always make things more painful. Reformers can create a sense of urgency to motivate change. In Nigeria, for example, people were shocked when reformers publicized findings that 99% of lawyers agreed the judiciary was corrupt. In Mexico, reformers used the Enron and WorldCom scandals in United States to push through higher Mexican corporate governance standards.

In 2004, at the start of tax reforms, Egyptian Finance Minister Youssef Boutros-Ghali pointed to weakening government finances and said, "Doing nothing is definitely not the solution. The greatest enemy to reforms is inertia."

We know nearly 85% of reforms in top reforming economies took place in the first 15 months of a new government. But even without a new political mandate, reformers can achieve a lot by simplifying administrative procedures. When the government succeeds in early reforms, citizens start seeing benefits—more jobs, more resources for health and education. The appetite for further reforms grows. Unable to make legislative changes easily, El Salvador cut the time to start a business from 155 days to 26 within 2 years—all through administrative reforms at the company registry. Now they are working on the law. Reformers in Pakistan implemented administrative reforms immediately while preparing the ground for the more difficult and costly longer term reforms. One of Kenya's reformers notes, "If we had waited for laws to do a number of things we're doing, we would not be doing them."

Ask development agencies about reform strategies and they'll likely talk about addressing the binding constraint to growth or sequencing the reforms efforts. Ask a successful reformer and they'll talk about seizing the opportunity, any opportunity. "Reform is like repairing a car with the engine running," says Mahmoud Mohieldin, the Egyptian minister of investment. In Nigeria it did not take years of strategizing before reforming the courts. Ten months after a new attorney-general of Lagos State took office, 26 new judges were appointed, specialized commercial divisions set up, and judges' salaries increased. In another example, property registration was reformed in Georgia in 4 months following the Rose Revolution. The previous government had spent 6 years going through the motions of commissioning studies, consulting with experts, and sponsoring seminars.

The strongest opposition usually comes from within. In Pakistan, customs workers were unhappy with the introduction of more efficient procedures and tried to subvert reform. In Mexico, a prominent media tycoon lobbied for weakened disclosure laws. In Serbia and Bulgaria, the ministers of justice did not want to yield power to more efficient company registries. In Peru, a modernized collateral registry promised to help borrowers but threatened the business of notaries, who protested loudly and managed to derail the reforms. In several European Union countries, notary associations lobby against the adoption of electronic signatures—which has vast potential to simplify bureaucracy. (This may change: recently the European Commission filed anti-competitiveness charges against 9 notary associations.)

Once you design the reforms well, the next way to overcome opposition is with a smart outreach campaign: telling people these are the reforms we are doing and this is how they are going to help you. But most reformers don't spend enough time on outreach. Opposition builds and few entrepreneurs grasp how much easier life can be after the reforms. El Salvadorian reformers worked with the media to explain and build support for the changes. Other reformers bargained directly with stakeholders. In Macedonia, labor unions were at first deeply opposed to the reform. But once they were brought into the reform process, they worked with the government and employers to improve regulation. Key to making the reform work was including the unions in the drafting of the new law.

Sometimes, a reformer even manages to convince the opposition. In Serbia, study tours for bankruptcy judges benefited the reform effort as much as they benefited the judges: "For every dime we spent on the tours, we saved tenfold from not having to spend money on overcoming resistance from the judges. They were welcoming the new law instead of fighting it." One USAID expert said that the study tours bolstered the credibility of reformers in the Ministry of Economy, as judges could "feel and taste and smell" for themselves and were more convinced that what they were being told could be put into practice.

Reformers can also blame changes on outsiders. It is no accident that Eastern Europe is the fastest reforming region. Reformers there could push through controversial changes by saying that the EU requires them. And El Salvador used access to the MCA as a reform rationale.

Sometimes a reformer needs luck. A fluke of timing helped Mexico overhaul its securities laws, a reform that *Doing Business 2007* named "Reform of the Year." "We finished drafting the bill in March 2004, too late to submit to Congress that term. But instead of waiting until October, we decided to show it to people in the private sector," relates José Antonio Gonzalez, director general for Securities and Insurance in the Ministry of Finance and a key drafter of the new law. "Their input made all the difference."

All reformers gain from using indicators that allow them to monitor progress and change course when needed. In Nigeria, the National Judicial Council announced ratings of judicial performance in May 2006. Judges now know they are being monitored by an institution with disciplinary power. The poorest performers have already left the bench. In El Salvador constant customer feedback on ideas about improved efficiency was crucial in measuring success of the reforms and identifying what was still missing. With clients as the evaluators of performance, reforms quickly became more appreciated—and customer-orientation became more than a buzzword.

## Who benefits from reform

In Bolivia 400,000 workers have formal jobs in the private sector—out of a population of 8.8 million. In India 8 million workers have such jobs—in a country of 1.1 billion people. In Malawi, 50,000 out of a population of 12 million. In Mozambique, 350,000 in a country of 20 million.

Reform can change this, by making it easier for formal businesses to create more jobs. Women and young workers benefit the most. Both groups account for a large share of the unemployed (figure 2). Reform also expands the reach of regulation by bringing businesses and workers into the formal sector. There, workers can have health insurance and pension benefits. Businesses pay some taxes. Products are subject to quality standards. And businesses can more easily obtain bank credit or use courts to resolve disputes.

FIGURE 2
**High unemployment among youth, especially females**

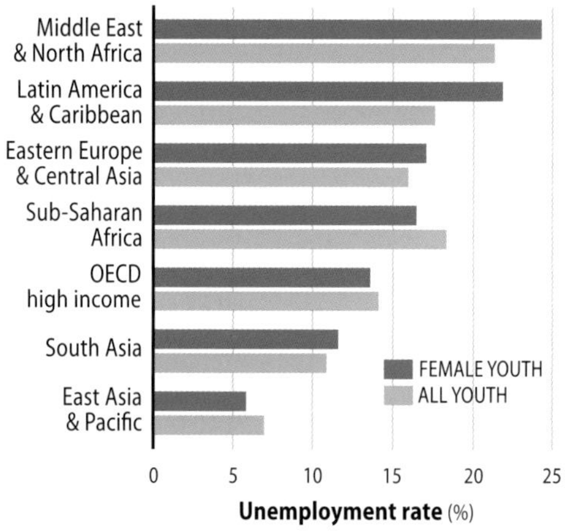

Source: ILO (2005).

Between 2002 and 2006 Slovakia's reforms have helped cut the number of unemployed people by 67,000. In Colombia reforms of employment and business startup regulations have created 300,000 jobs in the formal economy. Another success story comes from Peru, where in the past decade the government has issued property titles to 1.3 million urban households. Secure property rights have enabled parents to find jobs rather than staying home to protect their property. Similarly, children can now attend school. As a result, the incidence of child labor has fallen by nearly 30%.

A hypothetical improvement on all aspects of the *Doing Business* indicators to reach the level of the top quartile of countries is associated with an estimated 1.4 to 2.2 percentage points in annual economic growth. This is after controlling for other factors, such as income, government expenditure, investment, education, inflation, conflict, and geographic regions. In contrast, improving to the level of the top quartile of countries on macroeconomic and education indicators is associated with 0.4 to 1.0 additional percentage points in growth.

The gains come from 2 sources. First, businesses spend less time and money on dealing with regulations and chasing after scarce sources of finance. Instead, they spend their energies on producing and marketing their goods. The association between reforms and business profitability is best seen in the increase in equity market returns (figure 3). Second, the government spends fewer resources regulating and more providing basic social services.

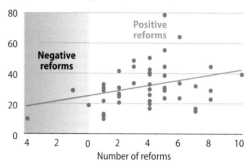

FIGURE 3
**More reforms, higher equity returns**
Equity market returns (percent, 2003–2006)

*Source:* MSCI, available at www.mscibarra.com, *Doing Business* database.

## What can development agencies do

If we were at the Oscars, development institutions would take a best-supporting actor award for several of the reforms described here. The large improvements in the business environment in Serbia, Macedonia, El Salvador, Guatemala were helped by the advice and attention of either the World Bank, the USAID, the MCA, or a bilateral agency like Sweden's SIDA.

For example, in 2004 donors included a reform of business registration in the list of 10 priorities for the new Serbian government. The Swedish International Development Agency was the biggest supporter of the reform. The World Bank and USAID commissioned several consulting studies, and Microsoft Corporation provided software installation expertise. The registry is now fully self-financing.

As another example, in November 2005 the Ministry of Finance of Mexico made an all-out effort to shepherd a new securities law through Congress. But opponents offered amendments that would affect 4 key provisions of the bill—amendments that would eviscerate the law's small investor protections. To help make the case for reform, Finance Minister Diaz asked the World Bank's *Doing Business* team to use its "protecting investors" indicators and benchmark the draft proposed by the government against the existing law and against the watered-down alternative proposed by a prominent tycoon.

The results were striking. Under the existing law, Mexico ranked 125 of 145 countries measured by the *Doing Business* investor protection index, with some of the weakest protections in the world for minority shareholders. Among Latin American countries measured, only Honduras and Venezuela had weaker investor protection.

If Mexico passed the law as presented by the Ministry of Finance, Mexico would shoot up the ranking index 92 places—to 33. Under the alternative law, Mexico's rank would have fallen to 132. "The simulations stirred enormous interest in Congress and in the media by showing the dramatic differences in Mexico's business environment if the law were not adopted," says one Ministry of Finance official. "If approved as proposed by the government, the new law would enhance investor protection and foster investment in publicly traded and even privately held companies. But if the changes proposed by the outside group were accepted, the opposite would happen."

Money sometimes helps: to finance new computers and refurbish courts or more generally provide the government with space to "buy out" opponents of reforms. But most reforms to business regulation aren't expensive. The Serbian business start-up reforms cost €2 million. Transforming Macedonia's labor laws cost only the time of legal drafters. El Salvadorian reformers spent only $90,000. Instead, donors help by bringing in relevant experience from other countries and by keeping the political determination of the government unwavering.

Perhaps the biggest contribution development agencies can make is to benchmark reform progress. Publishing comparative data on the ease of doing business inspires governments to reform. Since its start in October 2003, the *Doing Business* project has inspired or informed 107 reforms around the world. Mozambique is reforming several aspects of its business environment, with the goal of reaching the top rank on the ease of doing business in southern Africa. Burkina Faso, Mali and Niger are competing for the top rank in West Africa. Georgia has targeted the top 25 list and uses *Doing Business* indicators as benchmarks of its progress. Mauritius and Saudi Arabia have targeted the top 10.

Comparisons among states or cities within a country are even stronger drivers of reform. Recent studies across 13 cities in Brazil and 12 in Mexico have created fierce competition to build the best business environment. The reason is simple: with identical federal regulations, mayors have difficulty explaining why it takes longer or costs more to start a business or register property in their city. There are no excuses.

To be useful for reformers, indicators need to be simple, easy to replicate and linked to specific policy changes. Only then will they motivate reform and be useful in evaluating its success. Few such measures exist. But this is changing. In several countries, from Turkey to Mali and Mozambique, private businesses now participate in identifying the most needed reforms. Used to bottom lines, they bring a renewed focus on measurement. The culture of bureaucrats telling bureaucrats what's good for business is disappearing. Going with it is the aversion to measuring the results of regulatory reforms.

# Starting a business (quickly) in El Salvador

James Newton, Sylvia Solf, and Adriana Vicentini

On 24 January 2006 President Antonio Saca announced the launch of the new one-stop shop at the Commercial Registry, combining 8 startup procedures into 1. Starting a business, which took 115 days before reform, now took only 26. The next day the vice president cut the ribbon at the business registry site. Things were going well, thanks to a 4-year effort. "Everything can be done in 1 place now," says Felix Safie, director of the National Central Registry.

Starting a business, often the first contact between the entrepreneur and the government, was intimidating before the reforms. It took a lot of time and money—115 days and more than $2,700 in fees, plus $2,850 that had to be paid upfront as minimum capital. This, for a country with average income per capita of $2,145. It was not uncommon for a senior manager to spend 10 hours a day dealing with administrative formalities. Not surprisingly, 38% of entrepreneurs simply started their business informally, never registering or paying taxes.

This meant less revenue for the government, less protection for consumers, and no social security benefits for employees. It also meant that companies usually stayed small. Investing in new machinery or a bigger office building was difficult without access to bank loans. And then there was the constant worry of being discovered by the authorities.

Pressure started rising after several studies highlighted the issue. In addition, the complex startup procedures prevented El Salvador from qualifying for funding from the U.S. Millennium Challenge Account. Funds went only to countries that demonstrated above-average performance on several policy and economic indicators, including the time and cost to start a business. Something had to be done.

Safie decided to act. Since he had been called by the president to head the Central Registry in 1999, he had already reformed the property registry. Now he focused on the company registry. A former business owner, he knew that the way to change was to shift the focus from what bureaucrats wanted to what customers needed. In 2001 a human resource consultancy, HG Consultores, studied the registry's organization and recommended that it become ISO-certified. This meant complying with a series of standards for quality assurance in client service. Safie liked the idea. It would give the reform a specific target.

## Laying the groundwork for change

The ISO process offered a simple target for the reform, based on the motto "what gets measured gets done." First, "say what you do," that is, document procedures for work affecting product or service quality. Second, "do what you say," meaning retain records of the activities to measure and record compliance. Third, "improve what you do" by comparing set goals and actual results, and correct the problems that cause the differences. In February 2003 working groups were

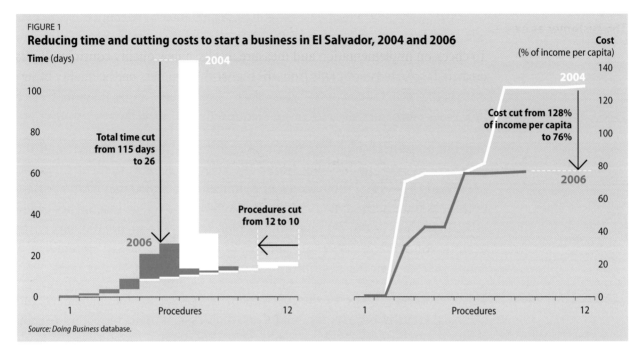

FIGURE 1

**Reducing time and cutting costs to start a business in El Salvador, 2004 and 2006**

formed to analyze 3 lines of work: company documentation (such as commercial registration), the business license, and the registration of the initial balance. "This review process is what took the most time, almost a whole year," remembers Manuel del Valle, whom Safie nominated as the new director of the Commercial Registry in June 2003, "but the bulk of the work was done."

And since most of it was done in-house, costs were low. Outside experts on ISO standards provided some initial training and guidance, but soon the registry's employees took over. They also wrote the new ISO manual (Documentación de Sistema de Gestión de la Calidad or Quality Management System Documentation). It outlined for all employees a narrative and schematic map to guide them through their and (everyone else's) processes within the registry. The guidelines also specified how to correct mistakes and make sure that they are not repeated. Each employee has a copy of the manual and is able to refer to it. Monthly meetings reassess the rules. Any changes are published on the registry's website.

Once the baseline procedures were documented, the reforms started in November 2003. "Everyone had been involved from the beginning and was ready to go," says del Valle. First, the staff was organized into small teams. Each employee was part of a team according to his or her work stream and task (grupo natural) and a reform group (grupo de proyectos de mejora). The teams met every week to discuss their previous work week, what went wrong, and how to improve it. During the week staff measured response times and thought of ways to cut or rearrange inefficient processes. All meetings were documented with action items for follow-up the next week.

## The customer as evaluator

To check on implementation and measure results, a new quality control unit was created. It solicited comments from the registry's customers on the quality of service through written and phone surveys and a prominently displayed suggestion box. So-called mystery shoppers, different people contracted by the quality control unit, tested the friendliness of client service and processing times. The results of these surveys were used to see where further improvements were needed.

The efforts paid off. After a year of hard work the major bottleneck, processing business licenses, was fixed. The time to start a business fell from 115 days to 40 by January 2005. The original goal of 85% customer satisfaction was exceeded. In March 2005 the registry became ISO certified, the first in Latin America.

Things also started moving at the top of the government. In the presidential campaign of 2003-04, soon-to-become-president Antonio Saca promised to launch a program called Programa Presidencial—El Salvador Eficiente. The program would improve the local business environment by cutting red tape.

In the 1990s the government's economic policies had focused on ensuring macroeconomic stability. Successfully: the country recovered strongly after the end of the civil war. But economic growth slowed to an annual average of 3.9% in 1995–99, and 1.9% in 2000–04. Concerned about this trend, President Saca realized that macroeconomic stability was not enough. Red tape was tying down businesses and holding back investors, both domestic and foreign.

With an increasingly open market, competition was only becoming stronger. El Salvador had been negotiating the Dominican Republic–Central America Free Trade Agreement. In December 2004 it was the first country to ratify the agreement. If nothing was done to make doing business easier in the country, chances were that local companies might be overrun by fierce competition.

At the insistence of President Saca, Eduardo Zablah-Touche, head of the Technical Secretariat of the Presidency, developed a plan to eliminate, simplify, and redesign bureaucratic processes that adversely affect the efficiency and functioning of businesses. Both men knew what it was like to be a businessperson in El Salvador. Before being elected in March 2004 Saca lobbied on behalf of private businesses as president of the National Association of the Private Enterprise. Zablah-Touche had been director of various companies and started a few of his own. "The happiest moments are when a new company is born."

## How far can you get without changing the law? A long way

When it was time to start implementing the plan, the technical secretary formed several reform committees to focus on red tape for trade, visa requirements, construction and environmental permits, and closing a company. Every committee included relevant public officials and businesses. In October 2005 the Commission for the Study of Reforms to the Commercial Code was established to review the commercial code and simplify business startup.

Backed by support from the President, Mayra de Morán, the director of the commission, wasted no time. She wanted results quickly. She also knew that legal reforms took time in El Salvador. "Anything that Congress has to approve takes at least 8 months." Her solution: let's see how far we can get without legal changes, just by reducing bureaucracy.

Any procedures not explicitly required by law were first to go. Chances were that they made little sense anyway. For example, certain ministries required that photocopies had to have certain size margins, with additional notarizations to ensure that the copy was accurate. Only very few photocopy businesses in San Salvador could provide this service.

Next, a single window would be established to allow entrepreneurs to complete formalities with different agencies in 1 visit. Visits had been required to 5 different public agencies. This was not the first time the idea of a single window had come up in El Salvador. Already in 2000 a 1-stop shop (Oficina Nacional de Inversiones) had been created in San Salvador, with branches opened in Sonsonate and San Miguel in 2005. Entrepreneurs could submit all their documents, but the staff still had to organize the registration at different agencies. This took time. And many people thought that the service was only for foreign investors, though it was also open to local investors.

The plan was to put officials from the different agencies in 1 building. Most important, they would have the authority to complete any formality by being electronically connected to their respective agencies. Entrepreneurs would be able to complete 8 different formalities in 1 place—the company registration, the registration of the initial balance sheet, obtaining the business license, tax ID for both income and value-added tax, official invoice papers, social security registration, and the notification of the Ministry of Labor.

It was quickly decided that the customer-oriented commercial registry, with its modern technology, would host the other agencies. To make implementation quicker and smoother, the commission postponed its goal of introducing a single registration form, since that might require changes in agency computer systems.

## A busy November 2005

The Technical Secretariat coordinated the development of service guidelines with interagency working groups and informed the public about the planned single window. After a schedule was developed for reallocating the delegates to the registry, work began in November to bring all the relevant agencies on board and start implementing the reform. In 1 week a core group of technicians, legal consultants from the affected ministries, and members of the reform commission drafted the guidelines. A day later the technical secretary met with top officials of the Ministry of Labor and the Social Security Institute (Instituto Salvadoreño del Seguro Social) to persuade the 2 to reform.

It worked. "This was our great advantage," recalls Morán. "The technical secretary was not directly affected by the reform, but was linked to the presidency. We could play the role of mediator or push for decisions when the process got stuck." The following week, the reform plans were discussed with all institutions involved. Each institution chose its delegated officials, and technicians planned the computer connections.

In the third week of November equipment and people could be moved to the registry. To save time and money, delegates at first brought their own computer equipment. Formalities were done on site, with the information sent electronically to the supervising agency. "Thankfully, most of the other agencies were already computerized, which made the transfer and connection much easier," says Morán. Only the Ministry of Labor was not. But since a simple notification suffices, the delegate can stamp the paper at the single window and have the package delivered to the ministry at the end of the day.

On 21 November 2005 the first tests were conducted. A few days later a random client was asked to test the system. Based on this experience, the guidelines and system were adjusted. Tests continued in the following weeks to make sure that everything was ready for the official opening in January 2006. This time the commission made sure that the reform would not go unnoticed, planning 2 major launch events.

The reform spirit received another boost. In December 2005 El Salvador became 1 of 2 lower-middle-income countries worldwide to qualify for Millennium Challenge Corporation (MCC) funding. (The other was Namibia.)

On 24 January 2006 the president announced the opening of the single window together with the official launch of El Salvador Eficiente at the presidential palace. A day later the vice president cut the ribbon at the registry in the presence of high-level officials from the ministries.

And so, 3 months after the first meeting of the reform commission, the new single window was operating. Entrepreneurs felt the results immediately. With all agencies in 1 place, paperwork was cut by more than half. Just by having different agencies share information, 24 separate requirements were eliminated. "Before, I had to give a copy of the company statutes to each of several agencies. Now I just need 1 copy for the company registry and they pass it on to the tax authorities," says one entrepreneur. The total time to start a business dropped even further, from 40 days to 26.

In November 2006 the MCC Board of Directors approved a 5-year, nearly $461 million grant for El Salvador to stimulate economic growth and reduce poverty in the country's northern region, where more than half the population lives below the poverty line. The grant is estimated to improve the lives of about 850,000 Salvadorans through strategic investments in education, public services, enterprise development, and transportation infrastructure. Incomes in the region are expected to increase by 20 percent over the 5-year term of the program, and by 30 percent within 10 years.

"We have improved substantially the environment to do business in El Salvador," said President Saca proudly. "We reduced the cost and time for the government formalities. With the recent launch of the one-stop shop at the Central Registry for company startup, we reduced the number of days to register a business, reducing the cost by 67%. These efforts have been internationally recognized by the World Bank, which placed us as one of the top 15 reformers worldwide in the 2007 report and moved us up 4 positions on the global ranking."

## What made it work?

Reform can start on all levels, particularly when simplifying the bureaucracy. And it does not have to cost much. The ISO certification—including audits, training, and 15 ISO certificates—cost $66,600. Together with about $12,000 for external consultants and new equipment, this amounts to buying 4 Toyota Camries in the United States. As an added benefit, since the employees redesigned processes, wrote guidelines, and established new rules, everyone was informed, felt responsible for results, and took credit for the success.

But once several agencies are involved, high-level support and institutional backup become important. "One of the main reasons for our success was that the commission operated under the presidency," remembers Morán. "We had support from the highest political level. And since we were not directly affected by the reform, we could play the role of mediator or decision-pusher when necessary. Everybody knew from the beginning that the president was going to open the single window. This pushed the reformers to work even harder. And thanks to the attention from the president, there was lots of publicity."

When dealing with several independent agencies, the weekly decision-making meetings with legal and technical representatives from the agencies moved the process along and ensured that everyone was on board. Since all meetings and decisions were well documented and followed up, there was no confusion about what had to be done, what was expected, and who was accountable. Quantitative indicators, such as reducing the response time for all formalities at the single window to 5 days, set measurable goals, which gave everyone a clear direction.

Constant customer feedback was crucial in measuring success and identifying what was still missing. With clients as the evaluators of performance, they quickly became more appreciated—and customer-orientation more than a buzzword.

The reformers also realized that it was not necessary to have all administrative details ready to be effective. With a little creativity, such as cutting down on the number of copies required, paperwork was reduced by more than half, and the center could open within 3 months. To save time and money for buying new equipment, delegates simply brought their own computers.

In the end, all the effort paid off. When the Dominican Republic-Central America Free Trade Agreement came into effect in March 2006, it took 26 days to start a business in El Salvador, faster than in Chile, Belgium, or Mexico, and more than twice as fast as the regional average of 73 days.

Work still remains. Cost is still high, with 75.6% of income per capita in official fees and 119.7% of income per capita paid before registering. Outdated legal requirements remain, such as publishing an establishment notice 3 times in the official journal and a national newspaper, at 3-day intervals, instead of simply on the registry's website. The rules and regulations were felt even during the reform. "One of the biggest challenges during the reform was the legal review to check whether any regulations existed that would be violated. Thankfully, we always had the legal experts in every meeting," says Morán.

But with the momentum gained from the success of the administrative reform, the reformers have started tackling these more difficult legal changes. The company code has been reviewed. Among the proposed amendments are cutting the minimum capital requirement, making the publication of notices electronic, and allowing notaries, lawyers, and the commercial registry to legalize books to introduce competition and lower the cost for the service.

# How to double business entry in two years

Tom Jersild and Zoran Skopljak

At a government press conference in December 2005 Serbian Minister for Economy and Privatization Predrag Bubalo said, "The Law on the Registration of Business Entities has produced fascinating results." On 18 January 2006 the Serbian Business Registry Agency celebrated its first anniversary. At the ceremony Bubalo proudly announced, "During the first year of operation the registry set up almost 11,000 new companies, an increase of 70% from the previous year."

For decades, starting a business in Serbia was time consuming and burdened with unnecessary bureaucratic hurdles—the rules inherited from the communist past were not business-friendly. Some of the biggest problems: the $5,000 minimum capital requirement for starting a limited liability company, the necessary inspections before a company could start operating, and the commercial courts checking every document. Sixteen commercial courts were in charge of registering enterprises, and 131 municipalities dealt with registering entrepreneurs. The practice was so inconsistent that even judges in the same court required different documents. As one lawyer says, "I had to file the same form to the same court in 15 different ways depending on what judge handled my registration." There were even cases when the courts refused to accept forms filled out electronically and instead insisted on handwritten materials.

Reports from the U.S. Agency for International Development (USAID), Deutsche Gesellschaft für Technische Zusammenarbeit (GTZ), the European Union, and the World Bank identified business registration as a serious problem. And in 2001–02 consensus was growing that something had to be done. A report for the Ministry of Economy and Privatization prepared recommendations for reforming Serbia's enterprise registration system. This report became the basis for reform.

After the decision to reform, the driving force behind the effort was the Interministerial Working Group on Deregulation, which later became the Council for Regulatory Reform. It drafted the primary laws, coordinated their implementation, and established the registry. Appointed in late 2002 by Aleksandar Vlahovic, the then Minister for Economy and Privatization, the group was in charge of drafting the Law on the Business Registration Agency and the Law on the Registration of Business Entities. Not all proceeded smoothly. In March 2003 the Serbian prime minister was assassinated, and after several months of uncertainty early elections were called in December. But thanks to the working group's enthusiasm and persistence, continuity was maintained, and significant delays were avoided.

## Changing the laws—and establishing the registry

The reform had 2 elements. The first was a radical change of the laws, and the second was making the new system work in practice by establishing a new registry. Three laws were enacted—the Law on the Business Registration Agency, the Law on the Registration of Business Entities, and the Company Law. The first 2 established the registry and radically changed the procedure for starting companies. They also moved the process from commercial courts and municipalities to the new administrative agency, unburdened by old habits and inertia. Using the Irish system as a model, the system was centralized and accessible via the Internet, leading to far greater legal certainty. As one attorney says, "Now I can check in a few minutes if a company exists, what is the address, and who is authorized to represent them. Before, I had to go to the court for each inquiry."

Another very important change was the deadline of 5 days to register a company. If no decision is made in 5 days, the applicant is free to begin operations ("silence is consent"). This was a big change. Previously under Serbian law, the decision was negative if the relevant administrative body did not respond in the prescribed time.

For the company law, too, rather than amend the old law, a new one more suitable for a market economy was created. The new company law reduced the minimum capital requirement for limited liability companies (90% of all companies in Serbia) from $5,000 to €500 and eased requirements for establishing companies by making the rules more flexible.

## Out-maneuvering opponents

The working group organized workshops with officials from Irish and Italian business registries to produce reform principles for the government. And 3 public discussions were organized with stakeholders after the laws were drafted. The critical moment was when the government adopted "The Principles" in April 2003. Vlahovic and Minister for International Economic Relations Goran Pitic were the main supporters, while the Ministry of Justice was the main opposition. The principles described the main policy objectives of the reforms and concrete steps for implementation. Andreja Marusic, the leader of the working group, pointed out that "by adopting the principles, the government gave political backing to the expert work we did and silenced lots of opposition."

The original plan was to have the necessary legislation in place by mid-2003, and the registry operating by the beginning of 2004. But the assassination of the prime minister in March 2003 and subsequent elections delayed the registry's startup until January 2005.

The biggest opponents of the reforms were the commercial courts and the Ministry of Justice, which tried to stall the process and persuade policymakers to keep business registration in the courts. Business registration was a large source of power and influence for commercial courts, and so they opposed removing it from their activities. The Serbian Chamber of Commerce and the National Bank of Serbia also wanted it under their control. Thanks to the persistence of the working group and later the Council for Regulatory Reform, the reform was implemented as envisaged at the beginning. Almost all facets of the law were included in the final language. But the Ministry of Finance and Tax Administration retained control of issuing tax identification numbers.

The new company law faced much less opposition. From the beginning there was a consensus among policymakers, the business community, and academics on the need for change. Foreign experts, mostly funded by USAID, helped early in the process and at some crucial moments, but local experts did most of the work. Even though adopting the new company law was much smoother than establishing the registry, limited public debate left some deficiencies. One is that the minimal capital requirement for a limited liability company was not reduced enough.

## Costs of reform—about €2 million

While the company law was mostly prepared by local experts, international donors were important sources of financing. In April 2003 the Serbian government adopted the principles of reform in the Jacobs Report to meet conditions for a World Bank loan. In 2004 donors included reform of business registration in the list of 10 priorities for the new Serbian government. The biggest contributions were €1.4 million from the Swedish International Development Agency and $150,000 from USAID for computers. The World Bank funded a great deal of consultancy work, and Microsoft Corporation donated provisional software for the registry and other essential and timely support. The total cost of reform was about €2 million ($2.3 million). The registry is now fully self-financing.

Implementing this reform was not easy. A new institution had to be established and a new system implemented. Having a core group of professionals in the working group and the Council for Regulatory Reform enabled continuity during 2 different governments and freed the reform from political influence. But this political neutrality was sometimes damaging because politicians were not fully committed.

FIGURE 1
**How Serbia reformed business entry**

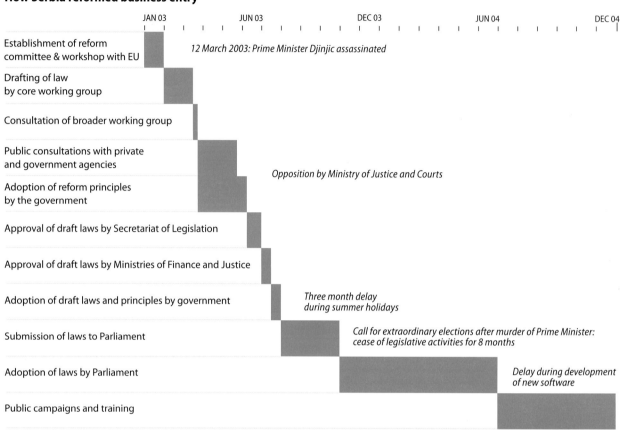

Source: *Doing Business* database.

After the laws were adopted, it was realized in the second part of 2004 that software and hardware purchases would not be made in time. As Andreja Marusic from the Council for Regulatory Reform describes, "It was clear that we were running out of time. We had 2 options—to postpone the start of the registry for a year and risk further delays, compromising the reform, or to start as planned and try to fix the problems as they came." The decision was to continue with starting up. The registry began operations at the beginning of January 2005 and a year later became the country's only address for business registration.

After the registry started the biggest challenge was re-registering existing companies, almost 70,000 of them. It was a big workload, and the commercial courts obstructed the process. In addition, the facilities were too small, but this will be fixed in 2007 when the registry moves to new facilities.

## Immediate effects—from 51 days to 18

The effects of the reform were felt almost immediately. The time necessary for starting a business was reduced from 51 days in 2004 to 18 in 2005. The new system was a radical change, with a focus on customer service and user friendliness. And the forms for registration are being continually improved to reduce the time to complete them. After the very decentralized and inconsistent practices of the commercial courts, the new system is centralized, with internet access to all registration data. To unify practices only 1 person—the registrar—has final authority and the power to interpret the relevant laws. This increases legal certainty and uniformity across the board.

During its first year, the Serbian Business Registry Agency registered almost 11,000 new companies, 70% more than in 2004, shrinking the informal sector. In 2 years, the number of registered businesses more than doubled. Praise has been high. One attorney says, "Since the registry started operating I did not have to appeal at all against their decisions, while before I had to do it very often."

## If it had to be done again

If Serbia had to do it again, it would adopt the principles of reform earlier to prevent delays and limit opposition, especially from the courts and the Justice Ministry. If reform implementation is assigned to a professional nonpolitical body, chances increase significantly that the reform will survive governmental or other political changes. Assigning reform coordination to an inter-ministerial working group, such as the Council for Regulatory Reform, accommodated various ministries that might otherwise have been in conflict.

Reforms should not be delayed because not everything is completely determined ahead of time. If the reform process takes too long, the risk is to lose momentum. Many issues are better addressed during the process.

Creating an entirely new institution with new specially-trained, more capable, and well paid staff, while somewhat extreme, helped avoid the legacy of prior institutions. Other options for a new Serbian business registration system were based on modifying existing institutions and procedures, but it is doubtful that they would have brought about the needed change.

Coordination with other reforms and legislative changes could have been better. For example, it is not possible to file registration documents electronically because the Law on Electronic Signatures is not in place. And other laws adopted were incompatible with the rules for registering a business.

Once the system is working, process improvements should continue to eliminate delays. And even though it was originally planned to have tax identification numbers at the registry, this still is not possible. The Tax Administration, more sophisticated and sensitive to various forms of tax fraud, is now scrutinizing tax identification number applications more closely. But its legitimate concerns for tax fraud should not delay business registration, so continuing efforts are necessary to improve cooperation between the company registry and other relevant agencies.

The business registration system in Serbia could be implemented in other countries. The Serbian system is not unique and was designed with European best practices in mind, the Irish model in particular. The Serbian example could be especially valuable for neighboring countries, which share similar problems and challenges. For example, in January 2007 the Serbian Business Registry Agency organized a workshop for Bulgarian counterparts who are working on their new registration system.

# Licensing 159 activities—not 909

Svetlana Bagaudinova, Dana Omran and Umar Shavurov

One October evening in 2004, Kakha Bendukidze, the minister of economy, and his deputy, Vakhtang Lejava, were discussing Georgia's byzantine system of construction licenses and permits. The construction sector was heating up in Tbilisi, but bureaucratic hurdles were weighing down on entrepreneurs. Lejava suggested establishing a one-stop shop and speeding up the process of construction permits by adopting a "silence-is-consent" rule.

Minister Bendukidze, a maverick reformer, argued that only a clean break from the past would do. This conversation led to the Law on Licensing and Permits and Regulation 140 on issuing construction permits, both issued in 2005. The result: the number of activities requiring a business license fell from 909 to 159.

## Prologue

The Rose Revolution of November 2003 brought in a government determined to reform and revive a moribund economy. Since 1999, the economy had barely grown and budget revenues lagged at about 79% of projections. The result was an increased external debt and some creative accounting techniques such as "forwarding" budget funds from one budget item to another and making fictitious budget offsets. In 2002, the International Monetary Fund suspended its programs in Georgia. This cut off the country from international capital markets, with external debt already above 50% of GDP. The following year budget revenues increased somewhat due to investment in the Baku-Tbilisi-Ceyhan oil pipeline; but expenditures jumped even faster. At the end of 2003, the total internal debt in unpaid salaries and pensions amounted to $120 million and half the population was living under the poverty line. It was time for bold changes.

## Over-licensed and under-monitored

Georgia had a complicated licensing regime typical of centrally planned economies. The 2002 Law on Grounds for Issuance of Licenses and Permits for Entrepreneurial Activities made some cosmetic changes to bring the regime in line with European principles, adopting the language of freedoms—that is, the free movement of people, goods, services, and capital. But the law did not simplify any of the licensing hurdles facing entrepreneurs. More than 900 business activities still required a license. Nor did the law impose any discipline on government agencies responsible for approving licenses and permit to do so in a timely and transparent fashion. Corruption was rampant.

These problems were most prevalent in the construction sector. A construction permit for a commercial warehouse in Tbilisi required 18 different procedures, including 9 approvals from as many agencies. Before applying for a construction permit, the builder needed permission from agencies as diverse as the Center of Archeology at the Academy of Science and the Inspector of Sanitary Observation.

The effect of such stringent requirements was twofold. First, they deterred many construction companies from complying with all the legal requirements. According to Natia Jokhadze, an official at the Ministry of Economy's Department of Urbanization and Construction, "The most frequent problem in construction in Tbilisi [was] the absence of project and planning documents and permits." Illegal construction activity was the rule, according to statistics from the Main Architectural and Construction Inspection Agency. In 2004, only 207 of the 484 ongoing construction projects in Tbilisi had permits.

Second, the cumbersome process meant long delays. Bribes became the way to speed things up. Jokhadze remarks, "After corruption in the police and customs, corruption in Georgia was most widespread in the construction sector."

The most striking example was the Main Administration for the State Comprehensive Evaluation of Construction Designs. Although a government agency, the Administration functioned like a private fiefdom with a monopoly on the approval of project designs. It required a "facilitation fee" to speed up the process, which could otherwise drag on for months. And the state assumed no responsibility for the safety of construction designs that the Administration approved.

**The super-reformer**

In the summer of 2004, President Saakashvilli invited Kakha Bendukidze to become Georgia's new minister of economy. Labeled as a "different sort of oligarch" by The Economist and as a patriot by the president, Bendukidze had the knowledge and drive to turn around the ailing reform efforts. At the time, Bendukidze was president and CEO of Russia's largest engineering company, United Heavy Machinery. In this capacity, he oversaw more than 200,000 workers and a budget larger than the state government budget of Georgia.

Bendukidze and his team started with an ambitious privatization program, but within a few months their agenda outgrew the confines of expanding private sector activity and generating budget revenues. In December 2004 Bendukidze became the State Minister for Reform Coordination. "I will be in charge of not only economic reforms but I will also recommend and oversee structural reforms in other sectors, for example in the Energy Ministry and the Agriculture Ministry. Of course, this does not mean that I will be responsible for electricity supply; I will recommend structural reforms which I think are necessary to carry out," said Minister Bendukidze in a televised interview in December 2004.

One of the first orders of business was a new law on licenses and permits. By all accounts the reform was entirely Bendukhidze's initiative. He commissioned the draft law from his team of experts and within 6 months it was ready for submission to parliament.

FIGURE 1
**Timeline of licensing reform in Georgia**

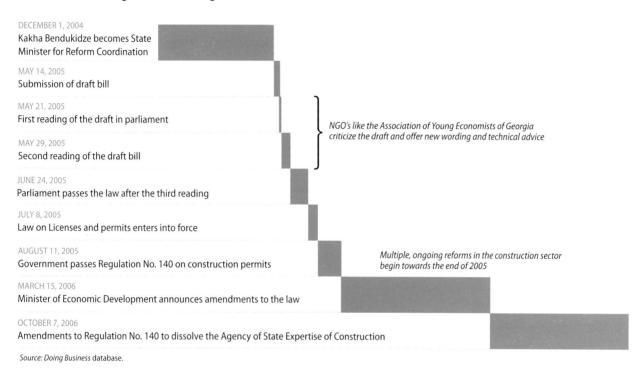

DECEMBER 1, 2004
Kakha Bendukidze becomes State
Minister for Reform Coordination

MAY 14, 2005
Submission of draft bill

MAY 21, 2005
First reading of the draft in parliament

*NGO's like the Association of Young Economists of Georgia
criticize the draft and offer new wording and technical advice*

MAY 29, 2005
Second reading of the draft bill

JUNE 24, 2005
Parliament passes the law after the third reading

JULY 8, 2005
Law on Licenses and permits enters into force

AUGUST 11, 2005
Government passes Regulation No. 140 on construction permits

*Multiple, ongoing reforms in the construction sector
begin towards the end of 2005*

MARCH 15, 2006
Minister of Economic Development announces amendments to the law

OCTOBER 7, 2006
Amendments to Regulation No. 140 to dissolve the Agency of State Expertise of Construction

*Source: Doing Business* database.

## Passing with flying colors

The Ministry of Reform consulted on the proposed reforms with the Association of Young Economists of Georgia, the Federation of Georgian Businesses, and a number of national experts. Most Georgian economists and businessmen hailed the draft law as an important step in Georgia's transition to a market economy. To quote George Isakadze, a prominent businessman, "Everybody agreed that country needed reforms in this sphere. The only difference was in the strategy—how to do it. This was a great start."

There were some doubters. The Association of Young Economists pointed to a number of provisions that were vague and which "allowed [for] different interpretations." For example, one expert, Ana Kadagidze, criticized an article allowing an issuing body to extend the administrative proceedings beyond statutory time limits as long as it notifies the applicant within 15 days of filing. She worried that this would allow government bureaucrats to extend the timeframe for licenses indefinitely, 15 days at a time.

As the Association hosted roundtables to discuss the draft law and distributed the resolution to its members for comments and consultation. In addition, they arranged three meetings between businessmen and the bill's drafters. The Federation of Georgian Businesses advertised the consultation meetings through television and other media outlets. "Many businessmen attended these meetings and expressed their concerns, but some of these concerns were not incorporated in the final version of the bill." Their main concern: that the lack of a license—a barrier to entry—would increase competition.

## A licensing revolution

It took three readings of the bill before Parliament passed the Law on Licensing and Permits on June 24, 2005. The law entered into force two weeks later. Its key benefits:

- Reducing the number of licenses required for doing business.

- Shifting many licenses to pure informational obligations, whereby a business can start operations and simply inform the authorities.

- Introducing a one-stop shop for licensing, "silence-is-consent" rules and statutory time limits.

The process of eliminating licenses rested on a simple question: "Why do we need this license?" All ministries and agencies had to show that their license was needed to minimize health, satefy or other risks. As a result, the law reduced the number of business activities requiring a license from 909 to 159. "And it's not over yet," says deputy-minister Lejava. The government plans to reduce the number of required licenses to 130 by the end of 2007.

The one-stop shop allows entrepreneurs to submit all their documents to one department, which is obliged within a month to undertake all required steps to issue a license or inform an applicant of the reasons for refusal.

If questions arise or additional measures are necessary, the terms of issuance might be extended up to three months or—if the government decides—up to six months. But if the entrepreneur fails to receive any answer within a month, this automatically means that the application requirements have been satisfied ("silence-is-consent"), in which case all responsibility is assumed by the state official who failed to do the job efficiently.

The new licensing law and the general administrative code (amended in June 2005) impose the following statutory time limits:

- 30 days after filing an application for a decision on granting a license.

- 20 days after filing an application for issuing a permit.

## Focusing on construction

The reformers solidified their success by adopting Regulation 140 (On the Terms and Conditions of Issuing Construction Permits) on August 11, 2005, only a month after the licensing law entered into force. This time the reform team consulted with the U.S. Agency for International Development on ways to improve the draft regulation.

Minister Bendukidze had previous experience in large construction projects and knew the specifics of what needed to be done—and how to do it. The reformers also knew who not to talk to. They fought against any institutionalized dialogue with large construction companies. Lejava says, "It would not have been productive to discuss these ideas with them and they would not be interested anyway. Our goal was to try to help the smaller firms so that we could reduce the entry barriers for them." Instead, the reform team organized several consultations to review the technical details of the draft with the Association of Civil Engineers, the Association of Developers, and the Union of Architects.

Unlike the licensing law, the proposed construction licensing regulations triggered fierce opposition. The Main Administration for the State Comprehensive Evaluation of Construction Designs opposed the idea of introducing private experts, which would eliminate some forms of state approval of construction documents—its main source of fees and bribes. After several months of vociferous

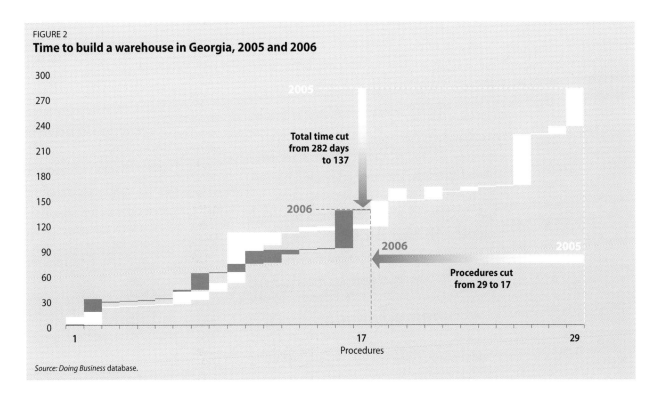

FIGURE 2
**Time to build a warehouse in Georgia, 2005 and 2006**

Total time cut from 282 days to 137

2005

2006

2006

2005

Procedures cut from 29 to 17

Procedures

*Source: Doing Business database.*

confrontations the Administration was dissolved. Private experts now evaluate construction designs—according to the old standards, until new standards are developed and reviewed.

In addition to changing the administration of construction permits, Regulation 140 reduced the number and type of structures requiring a construction permit. For example, buildings of less than 100 cubic meters no longer require a permit. Most important for small businesses, Resolution 140 simplifies the procedures and lowers the cost of issuing permits:

- It eliminates most of the approvals needed to apply for a construction permit. As a result, the number of procedures needed to build a warehouse dropped from 29 to 17 (figure 2).

- As a byproduct, the time to build a warehouse dropped from 285 days to 137.

The Ministry of Urbanization and Construction became the Department of Urbanization and Construction under the Ministry of Economy. Following the reorganization, the average salary of public officials in construction licensing was raised 20-fold—from a mere 15–20 lari in 2004 to 300–400 lari in 2006. Aggressive recruitment of younger experts increased the energy and vigor of the licensing administration. Meanwhile, more experienced officials were appointed heads of departments and divisions.

## The impact

Lejava is upbeat about the reforms, "Let's have a poll and see whether any of these companies would prefer living under the old regulations or the new?" The answer is most certainly the new.

Gia Kurtskalia from Magi Style, a construction company, remarks, "If I were a starting company, then I might have felt a bigger impact. The new law made life easier for firms operating without construction licenses. But for companies operating with all the legal documents, we felt no major changes. For the most part it seems that it should be easier." Data from the USAID's Georgia Business Climate Reform project suggest an increase of 151% in the number of construction permits in Tbilisi issued from 2005 to the first nine months of 2006 (figure 3).

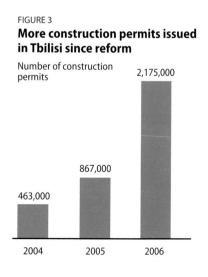

FIGURE 3

**More construction permits issued in Tbilisi since reform**

Number of construction permits

2,175,000

867,000

463,000

2004        2005        2006

The new regulations contributed to the further expansion of construction. To quote Prime Minister Zurab Nogaideli, "In 2005, the construction industry is the second most dynamically developing sector after the financial sector." Indeed, the share of construction in GDP grew from 3.7% in 2000, to 6.4% in 2003, to over 9% in 2006.

## Changing the game—but not the players

According to Isakadze, insufficient implementation momentum remains a challenge for Georgian reformers. The government did not prepare all relevant regulatory changes in time. And the absence of a communication campaign means that people simply do not know what the system offers them. Ignorance of the new laws, coupled with confusion, highlights the problems of "learning by doing."

The biggest problem is bureaucratic implementation. The one-stop shop for issuing licenses and permits is still a challenge, mostly because different administrative bodies lack effective electronic communication. Gia Kurtskalia observes, "It is visible on public officials' faces that it is still difficult. They have become more accountable, and we are not North America or Europe to make such a jump. There are day-to-day problems—computers do not work."

The silence-is-consent rule also had a mixed impact on issuing permits. After adopting Resolution 140, the government passed 10–12 amendments in quick succession. But the administration did not have enough time to train its staff. Without training and expertise, bureaucrats cannot keep up with the increase in demand. The result: if a negative decision is not reported to the applicant in time, the application is approved by default. This may still be a better outcome than having the building go up illegally.

The reform was not widely publicized. Until a recent publicity campaign, the business community, especially outside Tbilisi, was not aware that 85% of licenses and permits had been abolished. According to Isakadze, "More public awareness would have avoided the confusion the reform caused in the regions." Teimuraz Diasamidze, director of a company considered sizable and visible in the market, was not even aware of these measures, responding "which reforms?" Opinion is unanimous that a more targeted and effective public education campaign could have been launched when the law was adopted.

The reforms do not change the life of bigger companies significantly, as they have the resources to hire independent experts. But they do affect small and medium-size companies, responsible for finding their own experts for various preconstruction procedures. "Following the American example was good, and it will bring the Georgian standards up to the world's best practices," notes Tsagerali. But he is still wary of the drastic reforms that happened overnight. For instance, companies were stunned to go to the Geological Service and receive the following response: "If you know how to do a geological survey, go and do it yourself!" On the positive side, a bribe was not requested alongside this advice.

## Epilogue

According to Georgia's current minister of economy, Giorgi Arveladze, "Promotion and development of the construction sector remains a top priority." The government has identified three areas where it needs to enhance performance. First, it plans to launch awareness campaigns for small and medium-size enterprises by printing and disseminating information in plain language. Second, it pledges to ensure the proper administration of registration and permit issuance. Lejava says, "There is no magic bullet to solve these problems right away. Implementation of reforms in transitional economies lags behind the actual reforms. But we are catching up and will keep up." Third, it vows to concentrate more on enforcing regulations and punishing violators.

The Ministry of Reform Coordination plans to submit a new construction code to the spring session of Parliament. The draft code covers basic principles defined by the Law on Licenses and Permits and contains provisions for:

- Mandatory professional certification of specialists responsible for construction works, those working on construction sites and those servicing construction appliances.

- Professional liability insurance for specialists responsible for construction works.

Optimistic about the next chapter of reforms, Chogovadze says, "The liberation of the free entrepreneur from any restriction of red tape is the future of Georgia." Ever so bullish on the results of reforms, in 2004 Minister Bendukidze promised that the economic growth in Georgia will reach 12% annually by 2007. Three years on, many reforms have taken place and the economy in 2006 grew by 10.5%. Another successful year may make Bendukidze a prophet.

# Employing Macedonia's youth

Adam Larson, Kiril Minoski, and Janet Morris

The number of job contracts concluded in Macedonia increased 5.9% for January–October 2006 over same period a year before, with a 30.6% increase for fixed-term contracts—impressive gains for a country where unemployment hovered above 30% throughout the 1990s, partly due to rigid employment laws. "[Macedonia] wanted flexibility and we got it," says one local economist.

Macedonia passed the Labor Relations Act on 22 July 2005, the first significant labor law reform since 1993. Major reforms in labor and employment law are uncommon—largely because of the extraordinary political will required. Changing labor laws can inspire strong reactions from employers and employees alike, often in very different ways. Emotions can run high, with labor laws affecting something that both care about: their livelihoods.

With Macedonia suffering from chronically high unemployment, the government decided in 2003 that it was time for a major reform. Part of the cure was a new labor law that could better respond to the economy's needs. Passing the new law was a success for 2 key reasons. First, representatives of both employees and employers took part in the reform process. Each side had a voice, and neither felt excluded. Second, the new law enjoyed strong political support from both the governing and opposition parties in parliament.

While employers and employees disagreed on some issues, they agreed that a strong economy with low unemployment was a good thing. With that as a starting point, the government went to work.

## Chronically high unemployment

Macedonia had grappled with rising unemployment for decades. The problem was one of its most pressing social issues. Registered unemployment in Macedonia had been rising since the early 1960s, topping 20% in the 1970s. By 1991, when Macedonia gained independence from Yugoslavia, the economy had been contracting for more than 6 years, and unemployment was about 24%.

High unemployment hit Macedonia's youth and women especially hard. A 2003 study found that nearly 30% of the unemployed were between the ages of 15 and 24. In 2001 only 32% of Macedonian women of working age were employed, much less than 51% in the European Union and 54% in OECD countries. Nearly two-thirds of the people looking for work had been without a job for at least 4 years, and there was evidence that most of them were young.

**Fighting the problem at its source—the law**

Numerous factors contributing to Macedonia's soaring unemployment were beyond the country's control, but reforming Macedonia's labor law was a significant first step in combating unemployment. The Labor Relations Act of 4 December 2003 was principally based on a 1993 law (the Labor Relations Act of 27 December 1993), written mainly with socially owned and state-owned enterprises in mind. The government set out to pass a new law to address the changes in Macedonia's economy.

Reforms focused on 4 key issues. First, legislators introduced more flexibility in the types of labor contracts permitted and clarified the language of provisions governing part-time and fixed-term contracts. Second, they built more flexibility into overtime provisions. Third, they simplified redundancy procedures to make compliance easier and less costly. Fourth, they made changes to the collective bargaining framework, including those to comply with International Labor Organization standards.

**Making the reform happen**

When the Social Democratic Union of Macedonia won parliamentary elections in 2002, with Branko Crvenkovski as its head, one of its key election promises was to create jobs. Although Branko Crvenkovski left his position as prime minister to become president in 2004, the party remained in power throughout the reform process that led to a new labor law in 2005.

Aside from combating unemployment, the Macedonian government needed to reform its labor laws before it could join the European Union. The country had applied for membership in March 2004. The European Council Decision of 22 July 2003 set guidelines that called for member states to promote employment policies that would encourage job creation. It set the goal of reaching an employment rate of 70% by 2010. It also called for member countries to promote job creation by improving the adaptability of workers and firms to economic changes and restructuring—and by transforming undeclared work into regular employment through measures to eliminate undeclared work.

World Bank economist Arvo Kuddo advised the government throughout the reform process. He started in September 2004 by preparing lists of key reform objectives and proposing possible solutions to the government. Then between November 2004 and January 2005, labor and employer representatives had the opportunity to express their views on the key objectives through written proposals to the government.

FIGURE 1
**Timeline of labor law reform in Macedonia**

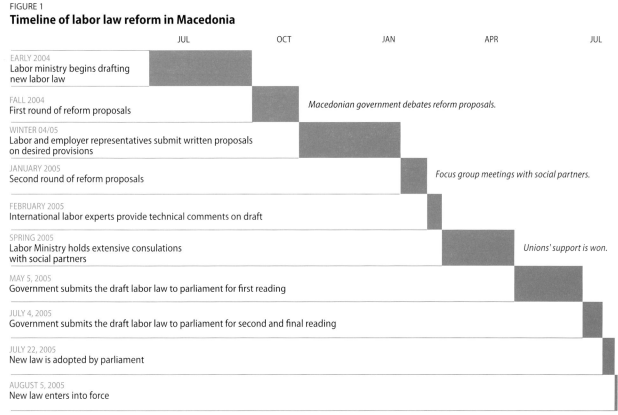

Source: *Doing Business* database.

In January 2005 meetings took place between officials from the Ministry of Labor and Social Policy and several "social partners" (employers associations, trade unions, and other interest groups). This was a crucial step. Participants shared their perspectives, voiced their concerns, and worked to hammer out a compromise. In March 2005 the Ministry of Labor held additional consultations so that the various groups could provide further input on the draft law. Throughout April and May the parties hotly debated a range of reform proposals.

Labor unions were at first deeply opposed to the reform. But once they were brought into the reform process and given a voice, they worked with the government and employer representatives to negotiate compromises. Key to making the process work was including the unions in the drafting, rather than crafting a law without their input. Through sustained interaction with the Ministry of Labor, the unions came to realize that reform was necessary. The new law was passed without disruptive strikes that might have impeded the reform effort.

The reform enjoyed support across the political spectrum. In fact, the greatest surprise was probably the ease and speed of parliament's passing the new law. With unemployment so persistent, the opposition party made a point of not challenging the legislation, and most parliamentarians genuinely favored reform. And its total cost was minimal, because there were no direct costs, simply the time dedicated by staff of the Ministry of Labor.

The government first submitted a draft of the law to parliament on 5 May 2005, and by 22 July the final version was passed. On 28 July the Labor Relations Act of 22 July 2005 was published in the Official Gazette of the Republic of Macedonia, entering into force 8 days later on 5 August 2005.

## Introduce flexibility, streamline, and clarify

The 2005 labor law created new and more flexible options for labor contracts, clarified and liberalized overtime provisions, limited the events that qualified for paid leave, and streamlined redundancy procedures. It also redefined the framework for collective bargaining, clarifying several rules and limiting the duration of collective bargaining agreements to 2 years.

Under the previous labor law, some articles were ambiguous, even about what types of contracts they purported to regulate. The new law clarified the rules applying to fixed-term and part-time contracts, and promoted more diverse employment relationships by loosening restrictions on the use of fixed-term, temporary, and part-time employment contracts. Article 46, for example, capped the total length of fixed-term contracts (including renewals) at 4 years, up from 3.

Previously, overtime was allowed only under exceptional circumstances, such as fires and epidemics. Under the new law overtime was no longer limited to those cases. Weekly overtime was limited to 10 hours, annual overtime to 190 hours, with lower limits for minors.

The old labor law required employers to notify a state employment agency each time a contract was terminated due to redundancy. Severance costs were high even by regional standards, with the maximum payment set at 8 monthly salaries. The new law relaxed preconditions for valid redundancy dismissals and limited maximum severance pay to 6 monthly salaries.

The collective bargaining framework under the old labor law violated ILO standards. Convention 144 on Tripartite Consultation required that representation by social partners be voluntary and that collective agreements bind only parties to the agreement. But Macedonia's collective agreements bound the entire public and private sectors, even workers whose representatives were not parties to the agreements. A single chamber of commerce represented all employers, whether an employer wanted to be represented by it or not. To complicate matters, the law did not provide clear rules defining which parties were qualified to represent employers and employees in negotiating collective agreements, and it placed no limits on the duration of a collective bargaining agreement.

The new law made membership in trade unions and employers' associations voluntary. It laid down rules for determining which parties may represent employers and employees in negotiating collective agreements. And the law made collective agreements binding only for signatories and members of signatory organizations. In addition, it limited collective agreements to a fixed 2-year term, making regular renegotiation necessary.

## Improving opinions—an important first step

For the government, the passage of the 2005 labor law was a great success. And understandably so: to have smoothly adopted a reform of such breadth was no small feat, especially with the divergence of views among the parties in the discussions.

Employers and employees alike are pleased with the flexibility the new law brought to employment contracts. "I consider the law positive," notes Slagjan Mihajlovski, owner of Infinite Solutions, a software development company with 20 employees, "because many of the obstacles to flexible forms of employment have been eliminated." Milivoje Dzordevic, the owner of fx3x, a visual effects and animation company with 20 employees, agrees, "My opinion of the labor law is positive, since it allows me flexible forms of employment [which are] essential for the nature of my project-oriented business. This is something that has a direct impact on the competitive position of my company." Twenty-year-old Marko Culev, a part-time employee at the company, adds, "[It] allowed me to have a part-time job, since I could work only 4 hours a day due to my various other responsibilities." He and other employees wish, however, that a public awareness campaign had brought the changes in the labor law to the general public's attention.

Some employers and employer representatives feel that more reform is needed, though they consider the new labor law a move in the right direction. Valentino Konstantinovski, owner of Etapa Project, an architecture and engineering firm with 6 employees, is pleased that the new law "shortens employment and redundancy procedures," but considers it "just the first step for establishing the overall framework that will support the growth of small and medium enterprises." Darko Velkov, owner of a private employment agency for temporary workers, Vrabotuvanje Leasing, and manager of the largest private employment agency, Vrabotuvanje.com (meaning "Employment.com") agrees, "[T]he new Labor Relations Act is a small movement in a positive direction, but it is just the first step in the adjustment of the legislation to the labor market needs." Mile Boskov, president of the Confederation of the Employers of the Republic of Macedonia, bluntly says that he supports an "ongoing process of regulatory guillotine."

Unions and employer organizations disagree over some of what they feel is good about the labor law. Labor unions emphasize that greater worker protections are needed, while employer organizations like the Employers' Organization of the Republic of Macedonia complain that the law is still too burdensome for the employer. While the quality of the legislation was high, the law was the result of a compromise, and as such, it probably fit no one's ideal. In the words of one economist, "The law is not perfect, but under the circumstances and the compromises that had to be made, it was a success."

But one point where both unions and employer representatives agree is their criticism of the minimum required by the new law for representing employers and employees in collective bargaining negotiations. According to Articles 212 and 213 of the new law, to take part in the negotiations on a collective agreement, union and employer organizations must each represent a minimum of 33% of the total number of employees and employers, respectively, covered by the collective agreement.

The problem in some situations is that no representative organization can meet this threshold. While this is not an obstacle to collective bargaining at the firm level, it is at the national and branch level. Macedonia, however, does not have a tradition of firm-level bargaining, so to solve this problem bargaining can either shift to the firm level, or unions can consolidate to join forces. Ironically, the high threshold was proposed by the dominant union as a way to protect its position. The strategy backfired, however, because even it fails to meet the threshold.

## Lesson—include social partners in the dialogue

The main lesson for other countries is that social partners need to be included in the drafting process at an early stage. Unions, chambers of commerce representing employers' interests, and groups of business executives all participated in discussions leading up to the 2005 reform. This gave them a voice and an opportunity to have their interests addressed, which led to broad acceptance of the new law.

Groups included in the talks are clearly more satisfied with the reform's outcome. Aco Spasevski of the Macedonian Chamber of Commerce, representing the interests of small- and medium-size enterprises, called the reform process a "positive experience" and made a point of emphasizing the concrete results of constructive cooperation with the government.

**Impact of the reform—an early indication of positive results to come**

Given that the new law makes it easier to form flexible labor contracts, it would not be surprising to see an increase in redundancies in the short term, followed by an increase in the number of fixed-term and part-time contracts. But significant layoffs have not taken place. Macedonia will need to experience both a period of economic expansion and one of contraction (a full business cycle) before the effects of the reform materialize.

An early indication that the reform is working is the rise in employment of youths ages 15–24. In the second quarter of 2006 (the most current labor statistics available) as compared with the same quarter in the previous year, employment rose 4 percentage points (from 13.4% to 17.4%) and unemployment fell 5.2 percentage points (from 59.8% to 54.6%). Because young people are the group most actively looking for work (as they are just entering the workforce), they are most likely to be affected by the reform in the short run.

Will the results of Macedonia's labor reform continue to be positive? The early signs are encouraging. The 2005 labor law was a critical move toward reducing unemployment. By consulting with labor law experts, building broad-based political support for the new legislation, and creating an effective dialogue with social partners, Macedonia has moved past an obstacle that impedes many countries.

# Need land administration reform? Start a revolution

PENELOPE FIDAS AND JIM MCNICHOLAS

You can bring a horse to the river, but you can't make it drink. This saying describes the futile attempts of development agencies to convince the government of President Shevardnadze on the need to reform land administration. The United Nation's Development Program first organized a seminar in Tbilisi in 1996 to discuss the need for improvement. Other donors soon joined. After numerous study tours, seminars, conferences and papers, the government was presented with a reform proposal in early 2003. In July the proposal was shelved.

Enter a reform-minded government in January 2004. Four months later major reforms are implemented.

## Private lands, public problems before 2004

Until the land-privatization program that began in 1992, most Georgian farms were state-run collectives averaging 428 hectares in size. Even under Soviet rule, however, Georgia had a vigorous private agricultural sector. In 1990, the private sector contributed 46 percent of gross agricultural output, and private productivity averaged about twice that of the state farms. Under the state system, designated plots were leased to farmers and town dwellers for private crop and livestock raising. As during the Soviet era, more than half of Georgia's meat and milk and nearly half of its eggs come from private producers.

The Gamsakhurdia government (1991-1992) postponed systematic land reform because he feared that local mafias would dominate the redistribution process. But within weeks of his ouster in early 1992, the new government issued a land reform resolution providing land grants of one-half hectare to individuals with the stipulation that the land be farmed. Commissions were established in each village to inventory land parcels and identify those to be privatized. Limitations were placed on what the new "owners" could do with their land, and would-be private farmers faced serious problems in obtaining seeds, fertilizer, and equipment. By the end of 1993, over half the cultivated land was in private hands. Small plots were given free to city dwellers to relieve the acute food shortage that year.

The Law on Private Ownership of Agricultural Land was passed in 1996. By then, nearly 4 million land parcels covering 930,000 hectacres had been allocated to 1.4 million households. But because of the high fee—26 lari for each parcel, or about $20—most new owners did not obtain sale-purchase acts. Land management fell to the State Department of Land Management, along with several other agencies whose responsibilities overlapped and sometimes contradicted each other. Decisions on land management, disposition, and registration were often delayed, confused, and swayed by bribes.

In 1996 Parliament issued the Law on Land Registration. But the law had a major flaw: the registry recorded only initial owners, not subsequent transactions. The State Department of Land Management tried to solve the problem but was overwhelmed with other tasks. Its mandate was too broad: design and implement programs for land valuation, land statistics, land registration and the cadastre, state control over land use and natural resources, development of state land management policies and legislation, and land reform, land arrangement, and disputes over property.

Other agencies further complicated matters. The Ministry of Agriculture and Food was responsible for agrarian reform, and the Ministry of State Property Management auctioned public lands. The Ministry of Urbanization and Construction shared responsibility for land-use planning and policy formulation. The Bureau of Technical Inventory kept records on real estate in urban areas. And the State Department of Geodesy and Cartography regulated surveying and mapping. Go figure.

The many functions of the State Department of Land Management created conflicts of interests. Land taxes and land-use conversion charges were based on land categories assigned by department authorities. Local political influence marred land categorization, dispute mediation, and registration, because the department's offices were paid by the local governments. Next, duplicate fees for services and conflicting property registrations discouraged the public. The Bureau of Technical Inventory, responsible for surveying and providing land cadastre sketches under the Soviet system, continued to conduct initial registrations, sometimes becoming a double registration system. Also, the Chamber of Public Notaries continued to be responsible for issuing non-encumbrance certificates, adding an additional step to already confusing procedures. Finally, both the State Department of Land Management and the Bureau of Technical Inventory were dependent on state funding, but they lacked the resources to fulfill all of their responsibilities.

Underfunded and marked by local power fiefdoms, land registration was rife with corruption. Low salaries, political influence, and poorly defined responsibilities and procedures created opportunities and incentives for abuse. Although agencies charged only nominal fees, "the actual price of land registration was determined by the amount of the bribe," explains Irma, a real estate broker familiar with both the old and new systems. Bribes started at $100.

Unqualified employees made matters worse. One study by the Association for the Protection of Land Owners' Rights, a Georgian nongovernmental organization, suggested that 40% of department staff were unfit for their jobs.

## Political will overcomes obstacles

The need for change was pressing. In 2002 the chairman of the State Department of Land Management convened a working group—including department representatives, international organizations, and local groups—to identify priorities. The Association for the Protection of Land Owners' Rights was active in the working group and subsequent reforms.

The working group built support for broad reforms. In early 2003 it submitted a concept paper to the chairman outlining the core objectives: to simplify and clarify registration, to streamline the department's functions, and to establish a transparent, self-financing registry through differentiated user fees. But the department was not ready for reform. Vested interests at local offices and in management feared losing influence over land privatization and administration. And the political environment discouraged risks.

"The starting point, and most important aspect of the discussion, was the political will to initiate reforms," explains David Egiashvili, then chairman of the State Department of Land Management. In November 2003 a rigged election brought thousands onto the streets of Tbilisi. They demanded change. President Shevardnadze was soon ousted in the "Rose Revolution," and a reform-minded government sworn in soon after.

On 25 January 2004 President Mikhail Saakhashvili took the oath of office, promising sweeping changes to make Georgia prosperous. Land reform and anticorruption measures were key to Saakhashvili's plan. In February Egiashvili became the new chairman of the State Department of Land Management. He convened a management team to oversee changes, including Tea Dabrundashvili, the first deputy chairman, and Nino Bakhtadze, head of the Tbilisi Registry Office. The Association for the Protection of Land Owners' Rights was a strong supporter from the start.

The goal was a new system to guarantee transparency and efficiency. The working group began with legislation and institutional reform. Drafting new legislation took 10 months. In June 2004 the Law on State Registry established the new National Agency of Public Registry, under the Ministry of Justice, to replace the State Department of Land Management and the Bureau of Technical Inventory. The agency was to be independent in its budget. In December 2004 the Law on Registration Fees for Services of the National Agency of Public Registry defined the agency's fees.

## The details of reform

The changes were dramatic. The management of the old department was fired. The information of the two previous institutions was transferred to the new agency. Employees moved to the new registry, but they had to apply for their jobs and take an exam to retain their positions. A massive recruitment campaign invited more people to apply. The exams were advertised widely.

The agency conducted more than 3,000 examinations, trimming the agency to about 600 employees, down from 2,100 at the State Department of Land Management and the Bureau of Technical Inventory. Salaries grew 20-fold—from 41 lari a month ($23) to 740 lari a month ($411)—which created a keen competition for positions. The Tbilisi Registry Office established an incentive system with performance bonuses, equivalent to 2 monthly wages.

Broad public information campaigns educated people about the benefits of property registration. And people trusted in the community spoke for the reforms. The Association for the Protection of Land Owners' Rights held public meetings, wrote newspaper articles, and distributed flyers. This initiative was important to success. The public responded with more registrations.

The effort drew on the ideas developed by the working group and international partners. No specific models were used. The Georgian system incorporated elements from the reform in Lithuania, and lessons from study tours and international workshops.

Development agencies, led by the German Development Bank, the German Technical Cooperation, and the World Bank, contributed expertise and technical advice, legal drafting, and equipment. The costs included capital, hiring, training, and the time to prepare and implement the transition. Capital costs—renovations, furniture, and computer hardware and software—exceeded $1.2 million (table 1). The costs of improving cadastre information, which now covers 70%–80% of the country, were fully financed by the German government.

The campaign was not without setbacks. Although begun in December 2004, staff recruitment was not done until August 2005. Frequent changes at the top of the Ministry of Justice also slowed reforms.

## Corruption down, registrations up

Everyone agrees that the reform reduced corruption at the registry. Jaba Ebanoidze of the Association for the Protection of Land Owners' Rights explains, "This is a combination of general reforms conducted by the new government, but at the registry agency specifically corruption has been virtually eliminated."

TABLE 1
**The costs of reform, 2004–2005**

| | Cost ($) | **Contribution** (% of expenditure by source) | |
| --- | --- | --- | --- |
| | | National Agency of Public Registry | International sources |
| Renovations | 836,036 | 36 | 64 |
| Software | 3,673 | 6 | 94 |
| Computers | 245,226 | 35 | 65 |
| Furniture | 154,708 | 100 | 0 |
| Total | 1,239,643 | 44 | 56 |

*Source:* National Agency of Public Registry

Lela Shatirishvili of Tbilisi Title Company highlights the role of differentiated fees and a new management culture: "That the level of service has improved and corruption has been reduced is obvious." Marina Khatiashvili of the Georgian Real Estate Association agrees, saying "Today, there are no bribes."

By 2005 revenues had already increased significantly, thanks to higher registrations, a new fee structure, and the retention of funds at the registry. People have become more willing to enter the property market, due in large part to the security of the new registration process. One goal of the reform was for the new agency to be self-financed through internal control of its funds. This was achieved in 2006, and the agency's fees now fund its operations. The higher salaries were funded by the higher fees collected at the new registry. And funding grew because of efficient services, with time limits and fees set by law.

FIGURE 1
**How Georgia reformed property registration**                              *Source: Doing Business database.*

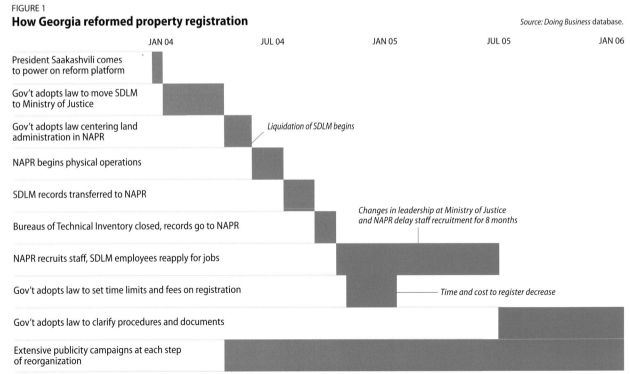

*Note:* SDLM is the Georgian State Department for Land Management, and NAPR the National Agency of Public Registry.

The procedures, time, and costs fell after the introduction of the National Agency of the Public Registry and the new law (figure 1). And optional expedited procedures, combined with lower fees and centralized procedures, put Georgia among the 10 least expensive countries to register property and among the 15 most efficient in the world, according to the World Bank's *Doing Business* report.

The government continued to reform and improve the system. The Law on Registration of Rights over Real Property, passed in February 2006, further simplifies the process and sets limits on the documents needed to register.

## How to limit the opposition?

Once the new government took office in 2004 the reform of the land registry faced little opposition. The government deftly minimized opposition by cutting registration fees and taxes and then redirecting them, appeasing both customers and the treasury. Although the 2% transfer tax was eliminated soon after the Rose Revolution, the registry lost no revenue because the tax previously went to the treasury. And because the treasury's losses were offset by increased revenues from other taxes, it did not oppose eliminating the tax either.

Key to the reform was dissolving the old department and creating a new agency. An overhaul of the old institution would have failed. It was too rigid and slow. New institutions with new mandates changed operations and mentalities—the services employees expected to provide and customers expected to receive.

For farmers like Erekle Katamadze, a certificate of registration has led to financial options he didn't have before. With a plan to buy a neighboring plot, Erekle expects to harvest an unprecedented five tons of grapes this season—four of which he will sell to winemakers. More importantly, Erekle and farmers like him are demonstrating an important aspect of land reform in Georgia: owning their own land encourages farmers to take responsibility for their own futures. "We're not just talking about the right to buy and sell land; we're talking about the right to manage our own lives," he explains. "Now we can decide for ourselves what to grow, and the profit gained is our profit. Owning your own land is an incentive to work harder, to live better."

Georgia needed more financial resources, so revenues were key. Its small size promoted a centralized information collection and registry system. Its limited technological resources demanded a simple documentation process. And its poor roads, electricity outages, and inefficient postal system required that services be available locally.

## An appetite for further reform

"The situation is better, but it is not enough," says Egiashvili. Recognizing that conditions and services at local offices are not consistent, the government plans investments in equipment and training. One worry is that increasing flows of registrations will pressure resources and challenge the agency's ability to provide accurate and timely services.

Recent tax reforms have had a significant benefit on the performance of agribusiness. Property taxes on plots of land less than 5ha have been abolished. The 2005 Tax Code provides also for the abolition of tax on transactions in property, zero percent profit tax and VAT, zero percent VAT on primary supply of agricultural products, and zero percent import duty on agricultural and other equipment.

Further ideas from the Ministry of Justice to implement these changes are expected. Zaza Bibliashvili of BGI Law believes that the system is moving in the right direction. "The laws are manageable," Bibliashvili says. "Now it is time for society, and members of the business community in particular, to demand improved services in these and other areas of the government." The Rose Revolution promised prosperity. And this can only be achieved with continuous reforms.

# Reforming the credit bureau law

FREDERIC BUSTELO

Credit is now more accessible for Panama's citizens and businesses, thanks to an ambitious reform of the credit bureau law. Many of Panama's 300,000 small and medium businesses—employing 68% of workers in the country—were cut off from credit before the reform. And more than 40% of Panamanian adults, mostly the poorest, had no formal credit, forced to rely instead on pawn shops and street lenders.

## Strong banking, weak credit

This was despite advanced financial markets. With more than 80 national and foreign banks, Panama has one of the highest ratios of domestic credit to gross domestic product in Latin America. Nearly three-quarters of formal workers have a bank account. The Panamanian Credit Association, the private credit information bureau established in 1957, covers about 60% of the adult population, more than twice the regional average.

So why the gaps in credit? Panama's 2002 law on credit bureaus forbade them from using scoring techniques or collecting information from utility firms, making it harder for poor people and smaller firms without bank loans or credit cards to build a credit history. And the system was opaque for consumers: they could see the information stored in the bureau only by requesting a report in person at the credit bureau's main offices in Panama City or in the City of David. "We were suddenly seen as the 'bad guy' who was denying credit to people," recalls German Espinosa, an officer at the Panamanian Credit Association.

## Turning opponents into allies

"The bureau needed to allow Panama's small businesses to access the credit market," says Luz Maria Salamina, the new director of the Panamanian Credit Association who planned the bureau's three-year strategy in 2003.

But not everyone in Panama agreed on the direction to take. In 2003 Osman Gomez, a legislator from the ruling party, floated an amendment proposing to erase all data within 30 days after late payments and defaults are settled. The amendment would make it impossible to differentiate between a borrower who always pays on time and one who often pays late. Consumer groups and several members of Parliament argued that negative credit records should not be kept, citing cases when an individual or a business person went through a bad period but recovered. So the Panamanian Credit Association held meetings with them to explain the benefits of retaining data even when debt was settled. The draft bill was later abandoned.

And in April 2005 Yassir Purcait, a newly elected legislator, made another proposal in the wrong direction. It would forbid credit bureaus from distributing data until three months after debt had become overdue. This proposal, by preventing financial institutions from differentiating between defaulters and non-defaulters, contradicted the objectives of a credit bureau. Again the Panamanian Credit Association stepped in to convince Purcait of the benefits of distributing the data immediately. Purcait proved receptive to their ideas, becoming an ally.

This strategy—turning potential foes into allies—became central to reform. Salamina says, "We needed to turn all these groups into advocates of our cause. If the Panamanian Credit Association says credit bureaus are great, we will never be believed; we need others to say so!" Because most actors did not know much about credit bureaus, the Panamanian Credit Association set out to educate them.

## The Credit Association's educational campaign

The Panamanian Credit Association targeted legislators—many of whom opposed the credit bureau in principle—and made tailored presentations to sympathetic groups of legislators. They also met with the party leaders, who led the debates and carried the votes of their followers. By the end of the campaign the Credit Association reached about 80% of the legislators, emphasizing the benefits to Panama's 300,000 small and medium-size enterprises, a significant voting constituency.

To boost its argument, the Panamanian Credit Association organized discussions with the powerful consumer and small and medium-size enterprise associations, which initially opposed changing the law because they feared the abuse of personal data. The Credit Association emphasized the benefits of bureaus for consumers demanding better access to credit.

The Credit Association's public relations campaign, launched in 2003, helped persuade doubters. The Credit Association got physically closer to consumers by moving customer service from the 17th floor of a high-rise building to an office on one of Panama City's busiest streets, doubling consultations with the public. It opened another customer service office in 2005, in a new mall next to the bus station. Consultations reached new consumer groups coming from the countryside, doubling again to about 6,000 a month. Consumers were educated about the benefits of credit information and received free credit reports.

By 2005 more than 100,000 people had visited the center. Getting ready to handle more sophisticated operations, the Credit Association also started improving its hardware, software, and technological infrastructure. Emphasizing its commitment to high standards, the Credit Association gained International Organization for Standardization 9001 certification in January 2006.

Involving other independent technical bodies, domestic and international, gave the reform credibility. Both the Banks Supervision Agency and the Banking Association were keen for credit scoring to be allowed because it would give banks better tools to improve the quality of their portfolios. And in March 2005 the Panamanian Credit Association invited the International Finance Corporation, the private-sector arm of the World Bank, to evaluate its operations and propose amendments to the law.

## The Credit Association pushes for reform—with help from new allies

The Panamanian Credit Association's strategy paid off in September 2005 when Yassir Purcait became president of the Commission of Commerce, Industry, and Economic Affairs, responsible for financial sector laws in the National Legislative Assembly. In October Purcait presented a new draft bill, heavily influenced by the Credit Association's ideas. The government's openness to new ideas and its willingness to hold discussions with stakeholders were keys to success.

In the debates before the legislative commission and Parliament the Credit Association held to its strategy—mobilizing sympathizers and turning foes into allies. The Ministry of Commerce and Industries fought an initiative to regulate the price of credit reports, arguing that this should be left to market forces. When a small group of legislators proposed cutting the time for keeping credit information to three years, the Banks Supervision Agency issued a written opinion that was crucial to keeping data for seven years.

The Commission for Free Competition and Consumer Affairs—a force behind the first credit bureau law in 2002—had long been an opponent of the Credit Association. But after the 2002 law regular meetings between the Credit Association and the consumer commission to evaluate complaints and design action plans to solve them built trust. The consumer commission was now very cooperative.

The Credit Association could mobilize all these actors and get their buy-in thanks to the credibility it had earned over almost 50 years—impressive, given that consumers and regulators easily become suspicious of a private entity handling sensitive credit information.

International support was also key in the debates. In November 2005 an Argentine expert from Experian, a global credit information company, made a presentation on credit scoring to the legislative commission. The Credit Association then sent a letter to encourage legal changes to allow the development of modern credit evaluation tools. Panama's high ranking in *Doing Business'* getting credit index also made legislators hesitant to take any action that would lower Panama's ranking.

Finally endorsed by the legislative commission in November 2005, the bill was sent to the National Assembly for approval. Debate on the final text started just before the Assembly started its annual recess in December.

The debates continued into March. Support for reform got a boost from a conference on credit reporting that the Credit Association organized to give the project a positive spin. The Credit Association was lucky—it had planned the conference not knowing whether it would take place before the vote. With more than 350 attendees, including many members of Parliament, the conference helped diffuse some lingering doubts. The International Finance Corporation's representative, Maddedu, was the main speaker, and the Credit Association held private meetings with legislators, the minister of commerce, and the powerful minister of housing. More than 29 different media outlets covered the conference, including 80% of the most popular television and radio stations.

After all the favorable media exposure, the National Assembly approved the law by a margin of 49 votes to 29. Indeed, the campaign generated such legislative and public support that even amendments not contemplated in the original draft, such as consumers' ability to request reporting from utilities, were adopted. The law was published in the official gazette on 18 May 2006.

## Deeper information, more transparent access, more advanced scoring techniques

The new credit bureau law improved the depth of the credit information system, the quality of the data in credit databases, and the accuracy of the risk analyses. First, the new law allowed entrepreneurs and small and medium-size enterprises to request the addition of information on utility payments to their file. This way, entrepreneurs and smaller enterprises, even informal ones, can build a credit history, helping raise their chances of getting formal credit.

Second, the law made the system more open and transparent by significantly improving consumer rights. Credit bureaus must now promote consumer education on credit management. And consumers are entitled to free and unlimited access to unofficial printed credit reports, requested in person at the bureau's customer service centers. They can also obtain an official credit report by any means that the bureau chooses, including on the Internet or over the telephone. Previously, reports had to be requested in person. The law also gave consumers a bigger say in the content of their files. Consumers can request that the credit bureau include their telephone, address, and other demographic information in the database as an extra tool to verify their identity and prevent fraud. They can also request that credit references stay in the report for longer than the seven years established by law. And they can insert explanations or complaints about negative incidents.

FIGURE 1
**How Panama reformed the credit information law**

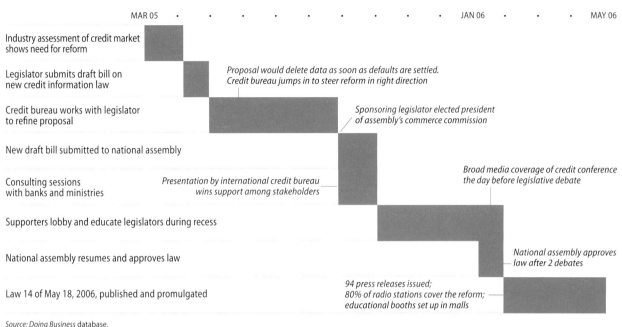

Source: *Doing Business* database.

Third, more advanced techniques were introduced for the analysis of credit data gathered by the credit bureau and for the evaluation of borrower risk. The law endorses the use of credit scoring, a powerful predictor of future repayments and a spur to bank lending.

## Still a long way to go

The reform of Panama's credit bureau law was fast—the new law was passed in a year. In Brazil, by contrast, reform discussions have taken seven years, and still nothing has happened. The quick passage of the law was the result of the Panamanian Credit Association's meticulous preparation. More than a year before the reform reached the National Assembly, the Credit Association had already initiated a consumer education campaign and was reaching out to legislators. This helped the Credit Association steer reforms in the right direction, gaining early support in the National Assembly.

The task now is implementing the reform. Consumers have already started adding comments in their credit reports explaining past incidents. More than 1,000 people did so in the eight months following the passage of the law. And the Panamanian Credit Association is setting up a new system for consumers to get their credit report through the Internet.

But credit information problems persist. According to the new legislation, utility payment information can be reported, but only if consumers specifically request it. This is cumbersome for consumers, and a big pool of data is necessary for credit scoring to be accurate. Only mobile phone information is automatically updated, because a release statement has been included in contracts since 2002. An automated process to handle information from water, electricity, and telephone companies does not yet exist, so adding information is still manual. The Credit Association plans to include a broader solution in the new proposed law on microfinance, including a provision for automatic reporting of utilities information.

Many challenges remain. The Panamanian Credit Association has chosen to develop a sophisticated credit scoring system from scratch, a completely new activity for the Association. It needs to develop new internal systems and to educate other financial institutions—accustomed to doing credit evaluation by hand—on using credit scoring.

How credit information tools develop in Panama remains to be seen. But with new finance reforms on the horizon, the pressure is now on the Panamanian Credit Association to show tangible results.

# Protecting investors from self-dealing

Melissa Johns and Jean Michel Lobet

A fluke of timing helped Mexico overhaul its securities laws. "We finished drafting the bill in March 2004, too late to submit to Congress that term. But instead of shelving it until October, we decided to show it to people in the private sector," relates a key drafter of the new law. "Their input made all the difference."

## Persistent underperformance

In 2004 Mexico's securities market was a tiny fraction of what would be expected from the size of its economy. The Republic of Korea's gross national income was similar ($600–$700 billion) but it had 10 times more listed firms. China had a securities market with 4 times the capital of Mexico's. Latin America received 9% of global private equity flows, but Mexico, with more than a third of the region's income, received only a tenth of that. And more companies were delisting rather than issuing new shares on the Mexican stock exchange. Investors looking for markets with the greatest liquidity, transparency, and shareholder rights were not investing in Mexico.

Why? Antiquated securities laws and tightly controlled companies gave minority investors little assurance that their rights would be protected. In 2004, Mexico had only 150 companies listed on the stock exchange, with 60% of them controlled by a single shareholder. A diagnostic report by the World Bank identified a number of weaknesses in the legal framework, including a lack of definition for directors' responsibilities toward the company. The law also had no requirement that subsidiaries comply with the corporate governance requirements, so not surprisingly many listed companies were holding companies, with subsidiaries operating outside the full corporate governance regime. It was difficult for minority shareholders—or any outsiders—to verify managers' financial conduct.

The result: insider deals were frequent, channeling wealth out of the company into the controlling shareholders' pockets. "There was a saying in Mexico: rich businessmen, poor companies," says one reformer.

## An opportunity to reform

The Fox administration's success in other financial sector reforms buoyed its hopes to improve Mexico's securities laws. According to one government official, "Earlier financial sector reforms were not very charged politically." Securities regulations were seen as another step in the administration's efforts to reform Mexico's financial markets. Congressional champions of reform were also vocal: one congresswoman challenged the minister of finance to attack vested interests in the securities markets, taunting him with the label "minister of stagnation" if he failed to push securities reform.

The highly publicized Enron and WorldCom financial scandals in the United States gave Mexican policymakers another political opportunity to push through their capital market reforms. Rather than rewrite existing legislation, the Ministry of Finance decided to draft a completely new act. The goal: greater Mexican competitiveness in the global contest for funds.

"Mexico has a huge need and a big appetite for capital investment," says one partner at a top Mexican law firm. Mutual funds, pension funds, and foreign capital in search of new destinations for investment had so far avoided Mexico. "There are funds in Mexico to go around. But without protection, people won't invest locally."

## A small drafting team

The original drafting team for the new law was small: a senior Ministry of Finance official, a senior official from the Comisión Nacional Bancaria y de Valores ("CNBV," Mexico's securities regulator), a lawyer from each office, and 2 outside lawyers. They started with a conceptual base drafted in October 2002 and worked through 2003 writing the new law (figure 1). Only in February 2004 did they complete a full draft for internal review. A month and a half later—a year and

FIGURE 1

**Timeline of investor protections reform in Mexico**                    *Source: Doing Business database.*

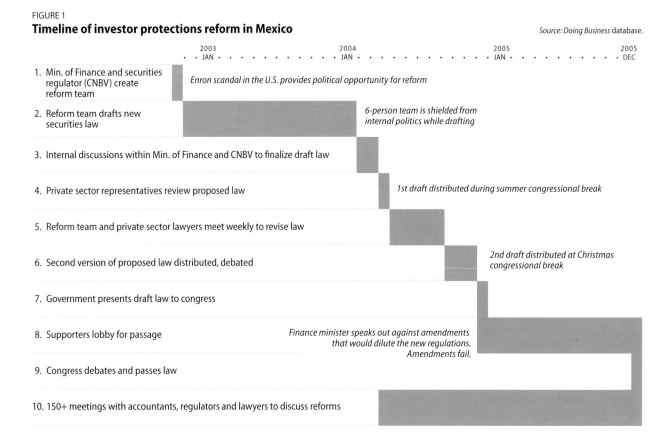

a half after beginning—the joint team was ready to present the proposed law to Congress. "We thought we were done, but it was only the beginning," says one member of the team.

The reform team's timing was off. In March 2004 Congress had only a few weeks until the end of the session. It was too late to submit such a large and important piece of legislation. But rather than waiting to unveil the bill in Congress and work through any opposition there, reformers took a novel approach: they invited the relevant stakeholders to review a "pre-draft" and participate in shaping it *before* submitting the bill to Congress.

This process took 2 steps. First, reformers met with every group that would be affected by the new legislation (business associations, finance professionals, the Mexican bar, the stock exchange, and listed companies) to present the goals of the reform. These goals were to strengthen the Mexican stock market through 1) new listed firms and 2) higher demand for Mexican firms' stock. As the government officials explained, the law sought to accomplish this through 3 approaches: 1) streamlined regulations for listing a new company; 2) increased transparency and minority investor rights; and 3) a corporate structure for listed companies that more closely reflected international best practices.

Second, after the presentations the reformers invited a group of prominent private sector lawyers, representative of all the groups, to form a drafting committee. This committee would go through the existing bill—keeping the goals for the legislation in mind—and eliminate any ambiguities, contradictions, and loopholes that might be found in the "pre-draft" text.

Ministry of Finance and CNBV officials met with representatives of top Mexican law firms every Thursday evening between 5pm and 8pm, April to September. "I call them the $15,000 meetings [the amount the attorneys would typically charge for their time]. In the end, we completely rewrote the law. And the final product met our goals—greater transparency of public company operations and broader protection of minority shareholder rights," says one official.

## The political battle

The political battle came next. The new draft was submitted to Congress in October 2004. Although its prospects were uncertain down to the final vote, it ultimately passed in substantively the same form 1 year later.

One of the biggest media conglomerates in Mexico was the most vocal opponent of the bill, protesting the minority shareholder protections and the disclosure provisions. The group also argued that the new law was too sophisticated for Mexico and too closely matched the United States' Sarbanes-Oxley legislation.

At one point it seemed the reform effort would fail. In November 2005 the Ministry of Finance made an all-out effort to shepherd the draft securities law through Congress. But opponents offered amendments that would affect 4 key provisions of the bill—amendments that would eviscerate the law's innovative protections. And the opponents were adept at using their access to the Mexican media to squelch support for the bill.

To help make the case for the complete law without amendments to the Congress, Finance Minister Diaz pulled in the World Bank's *Doing Business* team. Diaz asked the team to use its "protecting investors" indicators to benchmark the draft securities law proposed by the government against the existing law and against the watered-down alternative.

The results were striking. Under the existing law, Mexico ranked 125 out of 145 countries measured by the *Doing Business* investor protection index, with some of the weakest protections in the world for minority shareholders. Among Latin American countries measured, only Honduras and Venezuela had weaker investor protection.

If Mexico passed the law as presented by the Ministry of Finance, Mexico would shoot up the ranking index 92 spots—to 33. "Since we're the 20th largest economy in the world, we thought we should be ranked around 20 on the *Doing Business* rankings. But even with the improvement, we still hover in the 30s. We still have work to do," said one Ministry of Finance official. Under the alternative law, Mexico's rank would fall to 132.

## Disclosure and director liability—two key provisions

The difference hinged on disclosure and director liability provisions. The law proposed by the government strengthened disclosure requirements for directors who face a conflict of interest in their dealings with the firm. It also broadened the company's responsibility to report any transactions with company insiders. And the law made it easier for shareholders to hold directors accountable for actions harming the company. Mexico's performance on the *Doing Business* "extent of disclosure index" under the proposed law would increase from 6 to 8 (on a scale of 0 to 10), and its score on the

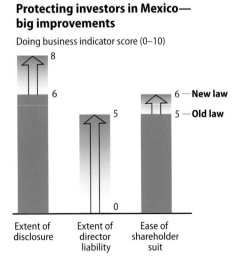

FIGURE 2

**Protecting investors in Mexico— big improvements**

Doing business indicator score (0–10)

"extent of director liability" would rise from 0 to 5 (figure 2).

With the proposed amendments, however, Mexico's performance on the "extent of disclosure index" would slide backwards significantly. The opponents' bill removed all requirements for a company to report large transactions with a director or controlling shareholder immediately to the marketplace and in the annual report. It also removed any obligation for the director or controlling shareholder to disclose a conflict of interest to the board.

Minister Diaz presented these results to Congress, along with myriad other reasons to pass the new law untouched. "The simulations stirred enormous interest in Congress and in the media by showing the dramatic differences in Mexico's business environment if the law were not adopted," says one of the bill's proponents. "If approved as proposed by the government, the new law would enhance investor protection and foster investment in publicly traded and even privately held companies. But if the changes proposed by the outside group were accepted, the opposite would happen."

The bill passed the lower chamber without the amendments on 6 December 2005 and was confirmed by the Senate a few days later. Heads of manufacturing and investment companies lobbied for its passage, thanks to the tireless work of the reformers to work with local business leaders and their counsel while drafting. The new law (Ley del Mercado de Valores) came into effect 28 June 2006.

**What does the new law do? Attack self-dealing**

The Ley del Mercado de Valores:

- Defines clearly the duties of company directors.
- Heightens disclosure requirements for related-party transactions (transactions involving a conflict of interest with a company insider).
- Requires committees of independent board members to review executive compensation and related-party transactions in publicly traded companies.
- Lowers the ownership threshold for minority shareholders to sue for damages.
- Formally establishes the subpoena power of Mexican regulators.
- Increases criminal penalties for corporate crimes.

The law attacked self-dealing. Previous legislation gave board members, directors, and shareholders broad and imprecise responsibility benchmarks. The new legislation presents 2 distinct duties for the board of directors of a publicly held corporation.

First, a duty of care. Board members must fulfill their duties in good faith and place the best interests of the corporation and the entities controlled by it above their own personal interests. They must attend board or committee meetings and disclose all information necessary to make decisions.

Second, a duty of loyalty. This duty forbids directors and individuals with decision-making authority over the corporation from diverting to themselves or to other persons a business opportunity that belongs to the corporation, without a legitimate cause. They cannot favor a shareholder or group of shareholders at the expense of others. Nor can they vote on issues in which they have a conflict of interest, or make inappropriate use of privileged information. Beyond these broad fiduciary obligations, the law provides a nonexhaustive list of activities considered disloyal and behaviors that constitute a lack of diligence.

"Fiduciary duty is the foundation that holds up the building," remarks one Mexican securities expert. "Before, the law was too broad and imprecise. It said you could do everything to someone, but in the end you couldn't do anything. It was a bomb without a fuse." The new law blended broad concepts with specific examples of what the lawmakers had in mind. The result, impermeable to loopholes, is enforceable by judges.

The new law also extends corporate governance obligations to subsidiaries. And finally, the law requires listed companies to set up committees of independent directors. These committees review deals involving senior executives, limiting executives' ability to use the company resources to fund lavish lifestyles or enrich themselves at company expense.

Lawyers enthusiastically greeted the greater disclosure for corporate activities and stronger standards for directors' obligations. "It keeps the proper balance between protection of minority shareholders and protection of the company from overly burdensome regulatory compliance," says one practitioner. "The main tension in the law is not a problem of shareholders in a pulverized market. It is more a matter of putting a minority shareholder on the same level as the large shareholders," added another.

## Introducing a new corporate form—the SAPI

The new law didn't only target listed companies. Facing a gap between strong corporate governance provisions for listed companies under the new securities law and weaker regulations for private companies under the company law, drafters sought a middle ground for larger private companies seeking a broader investor base. They found it in a new type of corporate form: one whose adoption is optional, but which offers enhanced corporate governance, minority rights and better access to the stock market as a way to attract minority investors.

That new corporate form is the Sociedades Anónimas Promotoras de Inversión (SAPI). SAPIs are stock corporations that offer minority shareholders the right to appoint board members, call for extraordinary shareholders meetings, bring civil actions against board members, and postpone voting with lower ownership threshold levels than in other corporate forms. In exchange for voluntarily adopting these provisions, SAPIs enjoy exemptions from the general corporations law to allow shareholder voting agreements, tag-along and drag-along rights, buy-back mechanisms for the redemption of shares, and restrictions on preemptive and exit rights.

Authorities hope SAPIs will bolster the low numbers of new offerings on the Mexican securities market by creating a breeding ground for listed companies. "Companies that adopt the SAPI regime will signal potential investors that the company is a good recipient of private equity with a credible legal commitment to honor the corporate rights of investors," announces one SAPI promoter. Even without an ultimate listing on the stock market, the regulators aim to increase medium-size companies' access to equity financing through the new structure without overloading them with complicated compliance requirements.

## The initial impact—balance, transparency, openness

Initial signs indicate that investors are happy with the new securities law. "Before the new law, investors were discouraged by the family domination of Mexican firms," says one Mexican lawyer who represents Mexican and foreign investors. "Previously, investors and joint venture partners had to battle for the 51% share. Lawyers had to be extremely creative to get protections for their clients. And we were never quite sure that the judges would uphold the protections we worked into the bylaws." Now local businesses and foreign investors feel the new law has increased balance, transparency, and openness.

This greater confidence is supported by market indicators. The value of shares and other equities on the Mexican stock exchange increased over the previous year by 13.1% in the first quarter of 2006 and 15.1% in the second— the 2 quarters immediately following passage of the new law.

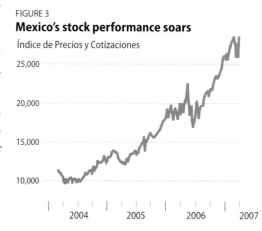

FIGURE 3
**Mexico's stock performance soars**

Índice de Precios y Cotizaciones

The market has continued to perform well over time: the IPC, Mexico's primary stock market index, shows a steady increase between passage of the new law and March 2007 (figure 3). The Mexican stock market also recorded a historical high in foreign direct investment, at $128,813 million, within a year of passing the law—a 20.89% increase from the beginning of 2006. And private investment funds in Mexico increased by 84% in 2006 over the year before. The many influences on investment flows make it difficult to attribute these movements directly to the new legislation, but such figures support the general argument that Mexico has become more attractive to investors.

Businesses are taking advantage of the law's innovations as well. More than 40 SAPIs have been created, voluntarily adopting stricter corporate governance rules to attract more external financing. The National Association of Corporate Lawyers, American Chamber of Commerce, Cámara de Comercio, Barra Mexicana, Mexican Association of Financial Law, Asociación Mexicana de Capital Privado, and the Asociación Mexicana de Instituciones Bursátiles have all held workshops on the benefits of the SAPI for companies and investors alike.

## Opposition continues

Yet opposition to the new law continues. As soon as it came into force, the media group that was initially the most active critic of the law challenged 54 of its articles. The group's allegations:

- The CNBV's new ability to issue sanctions prior to a legal procedure in front of the court violates the constitutionally protected right to be presumed innocent until proven guilty.

- The law's new duties for directors and auditors violate their constitutional right to work.

On 18 September 2006 a Mexican administrative judge found in favor for 3 of the group's companies, so the 54 articles will not apply to these companies until a final decision on the provisions' constitutionality. The provisions in question, if found unconstitutional, could be revoked for the entire populace. As of March 2007, there had been no final decision on the matter.

**Talking with stakeholders—priceless**

Despite this threat, lasting lessons arise from Mexico's securities law reform. Primary among them is the value of involving stakeholders early on in the process. "Through the drafting committee, business groups were able to make their points about the proposed regulations. And then we, as the regulators, made our points. In the end we came to common ground that served us well during the political fight," explains one reformer. "But you can't elaborate along the way with them," warns another. "That way you lose the pen. You must have the vision, present a complete draft, and take modifications."

Mexico's policymakers have since incorporated these lessons into major legislative efforts. "What we passed was too revolutionary to regulate by imposition," says one drafter. "The open, inclusive process led to a better law." He was clear on its value: "As MasterCard says, priceless."

# Adding a million taxpayers

RITA RAMALHO

Most tax reforms have one goal: increase tax revenues. Egypt is no exception. With a budget deficit in 2004 of £E40 billion, 8.3% of gross domestic product (GDP), Egypt had to reform. Finance Minister Youssef Boutros-Ghali said, "Doing nothing is definitely not the solution. The greatest enemy to reforms is inertia." Egypt did not stand still. After reform, tax return filings increased nearly 50% and income tax revenues grew as a share of GDP, even with rate cuts.

With 8.2 million people in the informal sector, 37% of the workforce, there was a great opportunity for broadening the tax base and increasing revenues. Tax evasion was the norm, with mutual distrust between taxpayers and tax authorities. Tax rates were high. Egypt charged 32–40% on corporate income, more than twice the 15% in Jordan and Lebanon. And Egypt was the second worst in the region in ease of paying taxes.

In July 2004 a new cabinet took office with a mandate to reform. One of its goals was to increase employment through investment. To do so, a high priority was placed on amending the tax law, customs law, and customs tariffs and on enacting competition and antitrust laws. Making Egyptian tax law closer to international practice would increase Egypt's competitiveness and its attractiveness as a destination for foreign investment.

The boldest reform would be to simplify tax law so that every business faces the same tax burden—with no exemptions, tax holidays, or special treatments for large or foreign businesses. Many tax laws start that way. But when hard times come and governments need revenue, they often raise tax rates. And large or well connected businesses usually get special treatment. Soon the tax law becomes riddled with exceptions, generally at the expense of small businesses, which have the least ability to lobby. This pushes them into the informal sector.

## Eliminating exemptions and reducing tax rates

Few reformers dare eliminate exemptions, reduce tax rates, and clarify tax rules. But Egypt did just this. In June 2005 the Egyptian parliament approved Law 91/2005. Now all companies are equal under the law, paying a 20% tax on profit (not 32% or 40%, depending on the activity, plus 2% as development duty). New tax holidays and special exemptions were eliminated, as was the state development duty. And the rules for multinational companies were improved. Egypt now uses a definition of permanent establishment based on UN convention; new rules for transfer pricing and thin capitalization are in place.

The withholding tax on interest and royalties was reduced from 32% to a 20% flat rate. The calculation of asset depreciation is specific in the new law, unlike previously, when the different rules to compute depreciation gave much discretion to the tax inspector.

The personal income tax was changed through the same law. The highest personal tax rate went from 32% to 20%. All individual taxpayers get an annual tax exemption of £E4,000. Benefits in kind, such as medical insurance, are now tax exempt. And the tax base now includes residents working abroad and nonresidents working in Egypt.

Taxation administration also improved. Self-assessment replaced administrative assessment, essential for the tax reform. As Boutros-Ghali says, "The point of the new law is to say what you want: whatever claim you make, we believe you, no questions asked, but you will be held criminally responsible and accountable for your claims." Under the old law, the taxpayer was considered guilty until proven innocent. Now the tax administration trusts the taxpayer.

The tax authority does not examine the tax return at the time of submission. Instead, the authority thoroughly audits a sample of taxpayers within 5 years of submission. A grace period exempted non-registered taxpayers from old taxes due if they registered and paid tax under the new law. And companies can now submit computerized records.

Under the new law there is less room for interpretation, reducing the possibility of negotiating taxes. As Ashraf al-Arabi, the senior tax adviser to the finance minister, says, "Bargaining is not in the deal any more." Replacing the old system of bonuses for tax collection for inspectors, the punishment for noncompliance was made more severe, and the accountant was made liable for the veracity of tax information. Under the new law, the accountant can go to jail for tax evasion, and fines can go up to £E10,000 ($1,839). At the same time, the tax appeals process improved to ensure that taxpayers' rights are protected. Taxpayers who overpaid are entitled to a refund within 45 days of the reimbursement application date. The goal of the reform was to make the tax administration more transparent and fair.

## Passing the reform

In July 2004 new reform-minded cabinet took office and one of the priorities of the new minister of finance, Boutros-Ghali, was to improve the income tax law. In late August the International Monetary Fund received a request to assist with drafting the new law. It took less than a month to produce the first draft. In October 2004 the government announced the intention to change the tax law to reduce rates and improve tax collection. It also started a media campaign to inform the public about the possible reform. By the end of October the law was finalized.

FIGURE 1
**Timeline of tax reform in Egypt**

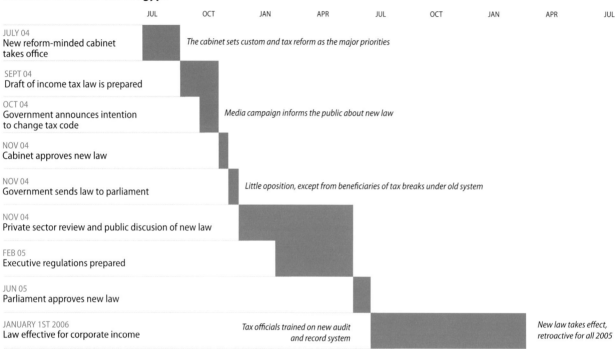

Source: *Doing Business* database.

The law was prepared so swiftly because the finance minister was committed to the project. In November 2004 the cabinet approved the new unified corporate and income tax law. The approved version was distributed to the private sector and to international organizations for review—and sent to the parliament. Roundtables were held with chambers of commerce, major accountants, and taxpayers in the 6 months before the law was passed in June 2005. The law for personal income tax was effective on 1 July 2005 and for corporate income tax on 1 January 2006.

The reform met little opposition. The public in general agreed that it was needed and was happy with the prospect of lower tax rates. The opposition came from the companies that lost their tax holidays (5 or 10 years of corporate income tax exemption). The major challenge was implementing reform. Along with the reduction in tax rates there was a major effort for administrative reform within the tax authority. Changing from administrative assessment to self-assessment meant a whole new way of collecting taxes. The tax administration was not very supportive because it was unfamiliar with the new system and thought that it had more control under the old system. It had to be convinced that the change was positive, done through training.

## More tax revenues—better economic performance

Over 2.5 million taxpayers submitted their tax returns, a significant increase from 1.7 million in 2005, in part because of the amnesty for tax evasion. This number may seem low in a country with 74 million people. But not all taxpayers need to file returns. If the sole source of income is wage income, taxes are withheld at the source.

Taxpayers with income other than wages must file a tax return at the end of the year to declare that extra income. So the 2.5 million taxpayers include only companies and the few wage earners with extra income from a small business. Tax revenues increased, even though the government expected a reduction. Corporate tax revenues went from £E22 billion in fiscal year 2004 to £E39 billion in fiscal year 2005, despite the fall in corporate tax rates (from 32–40% to 20%). Personal income tax revenues also increased, if marginally, from £E8.1 billion to £E8.3 billion, again despite the drop in rates. Overall income tax revenue increased from 7% of GDP to 9%.

Personal income tax revenues increased both for wage income (6%) and for small business income (4%). Much of the increase in corporate income tax revenue came from the oil sector, which experienced a boom in prices. This is still a positive result for the reform: the tax rate was cut by half and corporate tax revenues hardly fell. So the tax base must have expanded. More companies are complying with the tax system—more than a million more. The time to comply increased from 504 hours to 536 because companies are still adapting to the new system, taking longer this year to prepare, file, and pay corporate income tax.

Egypt's economic performance also improved. Growth in income per capita rose from 2.5% to 4.8%. Domestic investment went from 18% of GDP to 18.7%. The budget deficit was reduced and foreign direct investment increased.

## Learning from mistakes

Both taxpayers and tax officers will take time to adapt to the new system. The key is to keep learning from previous mistakes and improve the system. Furthermore, the tax reform is not limited to changing the income tax law only. An extra step was taken in May 2006 when the sales tax department and the income tax department were merged into the Egyptian tax department. With 1 tax authority to deal with, companies do not have to double their efforts to pay taxes. The government has also proposed changes to the sales tax law. The momentum of successful reform creates room for further reform.

The new law changed the tax collection system profoundly. Taxpayers used to be told what to pay. Now they compute that themselves. Some found it difficult to complete the tax forms. For instance, the form for companies with an accounting system is 46 pages long. Mistakes were common. Several sections of the form were left blank just because the taxpayer did not know how to fill it out. Nor were tax officers fully prepared to explain how the forms should be completed.

The solution was to extend the filing period to the end of July, then to the end of November 2006. The extensions allowed people to correct previous mistakes without having to pay a fine. The lesson: have more direct contact with taxpayers and answer their questions.

Prepare for implementation: the training of tax officers was not timely. It occurred in batches and new training courses were started even as late as October 2006. On the positive side, tax officers' lack of knowledge about the law was identified, and the tax authority is trying to solve the problem. The new law brings more sophisticated concepts, such as thin capitalization or transfer pricing rules, which are more difficult to implement.

The new residence-based system is more complex than the previous source-based system, so training is essential. A training center for tax administration will be operating in mid-2007. With the self-assessment system, tax inspectors become tax auditors. Rather than assess the tax due, they accept the calculation done by the taxpayer and audit a few taxpayers based on risk assessments. But they need training to become adept auditors. As of March 2007 a tax audit manual was still under development to help tax auditors. Lesson learned—prepare tax officers well, because they are an essential part of implementing the reform.

The Ministry of Finance first drafted and approved the law, then developed executive regulations to implement it. These regulations are a workbook that clarifies the new tax law, an essential piece of tax reform implementation. After that came the tax forms and the awareness campaign and training. The Ministry of Finance has learned that this may not have been the right sequence. Both the training and the awareness campaigns would have been more effective if started earlier.

**Still a long way to go**

Both the public and the government have a positive view of the reform. Sherif Hassan, owner of a medium-size business, says, "I used to pay 40% of profits, now I pay 20% and I do my own tax assessment. I don't have to wait for the tax inspector to tell me what to pay. Of course, I'm happy with this reform." The government sees better economic performance, higher tax revenues, and happier businesses.

Other countries can learn from Egypt's experience. The focus was on attracting new taxpayers into the system, accomplished by lowering tax rates, simplifying tax compliance, reducing the discretionary power of tax inspectors, and seeing the taxpayer as acting legally, but imposing harsh penalties otherwise. Other countries with large informal sectors can use this reform as a template for broadening the tax base and increasing tax revenues.

Mahmoud Mohieldin, the minister of investment, says, "Egypt has taken strides in the right direction by introducing these reform actions. However, we still have a long way to go, maybe another 15–20 years before Egypt can accomplish the more difficult task of eliminating illiteracy, improving health conditions, and introducing democratic governance."

# Speeding up trade

Allen Dennis

Trade is now easier in Pakistan, with customs clearance at the Karachi international container terminal dropping from 10 days in 2004 to 4 hours in 2007. Customs revenues are also up, from 115 billion rupees to 138 billion, despite a reduction in tariffs.

## Failures of earlier reforms

Customs reforms are not new in Pakistan. Indeed, computerizing the customs services started in 1979. More recent initiatives include an Express Lane Facility (1998) to simplify the examination procedure, an Electronic Assessment System (2000) to automate assessment, and a Risk Indicated Selective Examination (2002) to assess risk in the examination procedure. Other customs-related reforms include outsourcing customs valuation functions to pre-shipment inspection companies, simplifying and enhancing the institutional setup for the duty drawbacks, and bringing customs valuation into conformity with General Agreement on Tariffs and Trade Article 7.

Despite the good intentions, customs clearance continued to be cumbersome and slow. Clearing an import cargo required 62–113 steps and 26–34 customs officials. Clearing an export cargo required 31–46 steps and 17–20 handling officials. Not surprisingly, this left traders in Pakistan at a competitive disadvantage.

## Why the inability of the earlier efforts to ease customs clearance?

- The reforms were piecemeal. Clearing goods often required a chain of processes (declaration, valuation, examination, payment, and release). So tackling one link in the chain, even if effective, did little to shorten clearance times without attending to the other links.

- Key stakeholders were reluctant to participate. Traders expected that simplifying the duty drawback system would be less advantageous to them. Customs authorities expected that a new valuation scheme would mean large revenue losses.

- Political instability meant that in the 10 years to 2002, the average tenure of the chairman of the Central Bureau of Revenue, a political appointee, was less than a year.

- The turnover of key customs staff was high, hampering continuity.

- Customs operations lacked funds. Indeed, a fiscal crisis in 2001 prompted the reform of the Central Bureau of Revenue (CBR), the umbrella organization for Pakistan customs.

When President Pervez Musharraf came to power in October 1999, he appointed a reform-minded finance minister, Shaukat Aziz. Together, they pushed for reforms in several areas of the economy, with revenue administration being one of the most challenging. In 2000 the budget deficit was 6.4% of GDP, tax receipts were insufficient to service debt, and there were hardly any funds remaining for development. Further, the ability of the government to effectively deliver essential public services was under threat, and hyperinflation was looming. Reforming the tax administration was the single most important economic task facing the new government. It was not an option—it was a necessity.

## A task force to review and recommend

President Musharraf set up an independent task force in June 2000 (figure 1) to review the tax administration and recommend how best to improve it. Headed by Syed Shahid Husain, a retired World Bank executive, the task force consulted widely within the CBR and among various trade associations. It looked at all aspects of CBR operations, including sales tax, income tax, excise tax, and customs, and presented its findings in May 2001.

FIGURE 1
**Timeline of trade law reform in Pakistan**                    *Source: Doing Business database.*

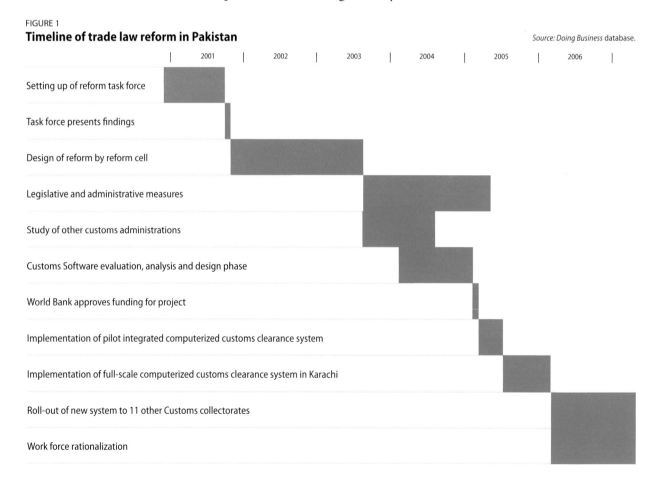

In a big departure from the past, the task force viewed customs not merely as a revenue generation agency, but as an integral part of economic development. It saw the major benefit from improving customs services in an improved trading environment, with reduced trading times, costs, and documents. Increased trading would create jobs, spur economic growth, and enlarge the revenue base.

The task force also confirmed the inadequacy of the piecemeal approach to earlier customs reforms. And flagging corruption, it identified serious problems in business processes and organization, human resources, and information management.

## A reform unit set up

The chairman of the CBR, Riaz Malik, was given the task of coming up with a reform program. The CBR reform cell had to grapple with several issues. Should the tax collection system be privatized, turning the CBR into a corporation? What should be the time frame for achieving the overall objectives? How should salaries be addressed? Should experts from the private sector be hired for specific assignments?

The reform unit received input on initial drafts of the reform agenda from the World Bank, International Monetary Fund, UN Conference on Trade and Development, and a foreign consulting firm (Maxwell Stamp). These consultations enabled it to assemble a comprehensive program to reform the CBR, approved in March 2003.

As part of the program the CBR's Customs Administration Reform (CARE) set out to redesign processes in customs operations and modernize customs services—through round-the-clock clearance, self-assessments, risk management, a paperless single-window environment, and reduced opportunities for discreet interaction between importers and customs officials.

As with the failed Public Revenue Authority Bill in 1998, the 2003 reform faced hurdles. Staff resisted change, fearing job losses from the rationalization of a bloated workforce. Staff also had interests vested in a corrupt and badly managed customs administration. Government rules and procedures reduced the flexibility that the CBR needed to hire private sector experts and offer higher salaries to CBR staff than to other public servants. Also needed was a legal basis for re-engineering the customs business processes through an electronic data interchange. That's not all. Possible political changes could remove government support. And several aspects of the reform agenda were expensive, requiring external funding.

## Start with quick wins

The reform cell strategy was to implement the short-term, less costly, quick-win reforms immediately while preparing the ground for the medium to long-term reforms, perhaps more complex and costly.

Among the quick wins was simplifying the documents required for trading—a simple administrative decision with very powerful consequences for the ease of trading. Traders needed to submit only 1 document, the Pakistan Goods Declaration. Other reforms followed:

- The CBR reduced the maximum tariff rates and the number of tariff bands, simplifying the valuation of customs duties.

- The CBR published a new professional code of ethics and conduct, signalling to staff the intent to eliminate corruption.

- To sustain the reforms, the Cabinet Committee for Finance and Revenue, headed by the minister of finance, and the CBR Board, were given fixed 5-year terms. The committee oversaw the CBR reform and reported directly to the president, thereby bringing considerable political clout to the reform.

- The legal basis for several of the medium to long-term measures was sought from the Ministry of Finance and the legislature. These included the CBR's ability to formulate its budget and administrative policies in specific areas, to have flexibility in spending its budget, to decide its compensation structure, and to adopt its own human resource recruitment and development strategy. Given the strong backing for reform, the necessary approvals were granted.

Envisaging resistance to costlier long-term reforms, the CBR adopted a proactive change management strategy, seeking to involve staff in the reform process by defining expectations, building consensus, and articulating a clear vision. Workers fearing job losses were assured that they would not be forced out of their jobs and that all workers departing voluntarily would get a "golden handshake." This helped reduce early resistance to reform.

## Costlier long-term reform

FINANCE. While implementing the quick win measures, a medium to long-term reform was also being prepared. The International Monetary Fund (IMF) approved a Poverty Reduction and Growth Facility with Pakistan in 2001, including tax policy changes and the CBR reform. The World Bank approved a project dealing with the CBR's medium- to longer term reform program in December 2004, with modernizing customs being a significant component. The $149 million project, co-financed by the government of Pakistan and the U.K. Department for International Development, is to be under implementation until 2009.

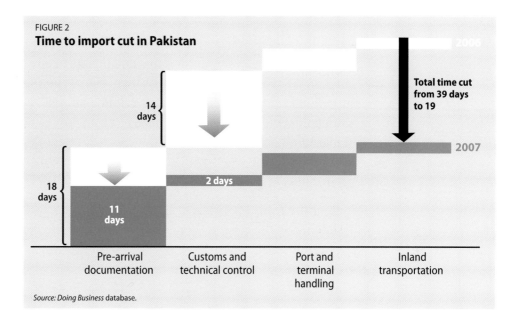

FIGURE 2
**Time to import cut in Pakistan**

Total time cut
from 39 days
to 19

14 days

18 days

11 days

2 days

2006

2007

Pre-arrival
documentation

Customs and
technical control

Port and
terminal
handling

Inland
transportation

*Source: Doing Business* database.

**Human resources.** A major long-term goal is to rationalize the workforce. The CBR is known to be overstaffed, particularly at lower grades. With a move to modern revenue administration, lower skills would be in even less demand. An improved compensation package for the reorganized CBR has been agreed upon. All staff are expected to apply for vacancies and those recruited will have a more lucrative package. New staff are expected to have higher qualifications, and the staff training program has been improved to build capacity. For staff not recruited, the strategy to reduce the workforce is voluntary and spaced over 5 years (2005–09). CBR officers with 25 years of service are expected to retire. And any surplus staff, particularly at lower grades, would be offered career counseling and retraining.

**Modernizing customs services.** Customs procedures are being modernized through the Pakistan Customs Computerized System (PACCS). Unlike previous standalone modules, the PACCS is a comprehensive integrated information technology system to implement user management, carrier declaration, goods declaration, risk management, assessment, examination, payments, management information systems, transhipment management, status notification, clearance management, adjudication management, security management, bonded warehouse management, and a tax node. The new system streamlines the clearance process (allowing for pre-arrival lodging of declarations, electronic payment, and signatures) and applies risk management.

PACCS was piloted in April 2005, and the electronic submission of documents was fully implemented at the Karachi International Container Terminal by January 2006. Traders can now lodge documents before goods arrive at the port, avoiding customs disputes because the system automatically determines the duty. Thanks to risk profiling (green, yellow, and red lanes), customs officials do much less physical inspection of goods.

The success so far (figure 2) is mainly at Karachi International Container Terminal, and is currently being rolled out to 11 other customs collectorates.

# Repairing a car with the engine running

Sᴀʙɪɴᴇ Hᴇʀᴛᴠᴇʟᴅᴛ

Commercial cases in the Nigerian state of Lagos can now be resolved in about a year—in stark contrast to the situation during 16 years of military rule. In 1997 the average duration of commercial cases before the court was over 4 years, and new cases filed in the late 1990s did not stand a reasonable chance of being concluded within a decade. People had no faith in getting justice through the courts.

Lagos started reforming the courts after Nigeria returned to democratic government in 1999. The governor-elect of Lagos, Senator Bola Ahmed Tinubu, promised to put things right. Immediately after his election in late 1999, he created a justice policy committee to review the entire legal system. The head of this committee, Professor Yemi Osinbajo, commissioned a widely publicized study that showed the judicial system to be suffering from rampant corruption and severe backlogs: 99% of lawyers polled agreed that the Lagos judiciary was corrupt. And pending before the High Court in May 2000 were 40,000 cases, with 10,000 new cases filed every year.

As soon as he was appointed attorney general of Lagos in June 1999, Osinbajo started reforming the entire judiciary, relying on strong support from Tinubu. Judicial reform in Lagos continues today. While some reforms were implemented immediately after the new government was elected, others are ongoing 7 years later.

## Corrupt judges dismissed

The 1999 Nigerian Constitution created the National Judicial Council, an independent body that can recommend the appointment and the dismissal of judges to the president and state governors.

Before 2000 no judge had ever been disciplined for corruption in Nigeria. To sanitize the Nigerian judiciary, the National Judicial Council instituted a review panel in 2001. Over the next 6 years it reviewed 130 judges, recommending 8 for dismissal, 15 for compulsory retirement, and 13 for reprimands. As of 2002, 21 magistrates and 3 high court judges were either dismissed or retired—the most thorough overhaul of the judiciary in Nigeria's history.

On 22 May 2001 the Lagos Judicial Service Commission appointed 26 judges from diverse backgrounds to the High Court, bringing the number of judges to 50 and reducing the average age from 55 to 44. The appointees went through a comprehensive 6 week training program, including legal, Internet, and computer training. In 2003 another 6 judges were added.

Appointing judges from various backgrounds—from universities, finance, and commerce—turned out to be a good strategy. Six years later, some of the most highly regarded judges are those with experience in areas other than courtroom litigation.

FIGURE 1
**Timeline of judicial reform in Lagos**

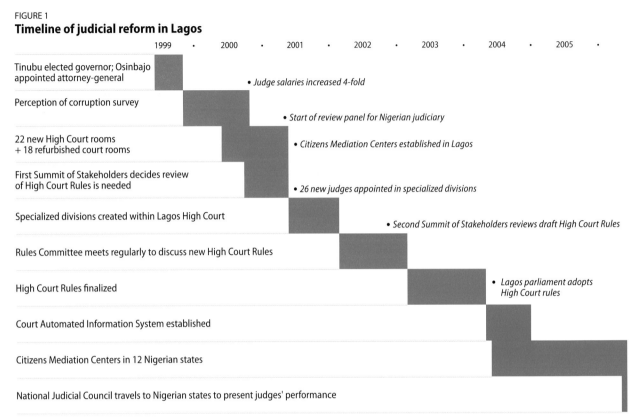

Source: *Doing Business* database.

To attract the right caliber to the bench and reduce the dependence on bribe money, judges' monthly salaries quadrupled from $600 to $2,400 between 1999 and 2001. On top of the salary, each judge receives medical insurance, a free vehicle, and a family house. A study showed that the greatest concern for judges is post-retirement housing. The compensation package now allows judges to lead comfortable lives. And since 2000, the National Judicial Council has given each judge an allowance of $1,568 for courtroom expenses, with auditors routinely inspecting expense receipts.

Also in 2000 and 2001, 22 new courtrooms for the High Court were constructed, and 18 were rehabilitated and supplied with computers, generators, and air conditioners at a cost of more than $9.6 million. A challenge then and now is electricity, with the fuel cost for generators running thousands of dollars a month.

In 2001, when the 26 new judges were appointed, specialized divisions were introduced in the High Court for commercial cases, land, family, revenue, criminal, and general civil matters. Each judge was appointed to a specialized division, depending on background and professional experience. For example, Justice Atinuke Ipaye, a former family law professor, was appointed to the family division. Justice Habeeb Abiru, a lawyer with extensive experience in property law, was appointed to the land division.

## New rules for the High Court

On 16 October 2000, the Summit of Stakeholders on the Administration of Justice in the 21st Century concluded that reducing delays and decongesting the courts would be impossible without reviewing the court rules. The review started in April 2002.

The 10 members of the Rules Committee were chosen from private attorneys, serving and retired justices, the Lagos Ministry of Justice, and representatives of the Lagos branch of the Nigerian bar association. Hurilaws, a nongovernmental organization of human rights lawyers, prepared a first set of draft rules, inspired largely by the U.K. court rules after the Woolf reform. The Nigerian Institute of Advanced Legal Studies then drafted a second set of rules. From April 2002 to early 2003 the Rules Committee met weekly and sometimes daily to review existing rules and to take the best ideas from the 2 sets to produce a final version.

On important issues, such as introducing pretrial conferences, a committee member was asked to prepare a separate memo to be discussed at the following committee meeting. Heated debates took place on contentious issues, such as putting a cap on the number of extensions and adjournments, which some committee members said would violate fundamental rights.

In early 2003 the Rules Committee presented its draft rules at the second Summit of Stakeholders. All key officers of the justice system were present, which was particularly useful in winning over a group of opposing lawyers. The Rules Committee amended some of its rules and finalized them by the end of 2003. In March 2004 the Lagos State Legislature adopted them without changes and in June 2004 the new rules entered into force.

## The new High Court rules include three innovations to reduce court delays and frivolous cases:

FRONTLOADING EVIDENCE. It is now mandatory for parties to submit all evidence they intend to rely on at the start of the legal proceedings. If the plaintiff fails to submit the evidence up front, his claim will not be accepted for filing at the court's registry. Because parties must submit witness depositions and copies of all documents they plan to use during trial, they are discouraged from filing frivolous claims meant only to exert pressure on the other party.

DEADLINES FOR ACTIONS. The 2004 rules specify timeframes to take certain actions. For example, defendants are expected to file a statement of defense within 42 days of receiving the statement of claims. The old rules had no timeframes.

**PRETRIAL CONFERENCES.** A promising aspect of the reform was the mandatory pretrial conference, an informal meeting of the judge and the parties to explore the possibility of settling the case amicably. The conferences also limit the areas of dispute and settle preliminary applications, such as challenges to the court's jurisdiction.

The 2004 Lagos High Court rules have served as a model for other Nigerian states.

## Automating court information

The Court Automation Information System started in January 2005. Justice Abisoye Ayo, a judge in the commercial division, has managed it since inception. Having worked in the United States for an IT company, she closely monitors weekly progress made by all 300 judicial assistants and court recorders, court registrars, secretaries, and computer operators inputting court cases and case events into the system over the intranet. The objective was for all litigation cases to be uploaded to the system by April 2007. In the near future, lawyers will be able to register cases and follow them online.

The system seeks to reduce case backlog and court delays, assign cases randomly, and calculate court fees automatically. More important, it will measure, manage, and improve individual and overall judicial performance. Case disposition standards, based on type of case, are reported for each judge. The system will also monitor the performance of judges against targets.

## Citizens mediation centers

As part of the Access to Justice Program, 5 citizens mediation centers, modeled on U.S. community mediation centers, opened in Lagos in 2000. In these centers, 38 trained mediators work to settle small disputes that would otherwise end up in the courts. The mediators are legal counsels, employed and paid by the Lagos Ministry of Justice.

The 5 centers in Lagos resolve disputes quickly, free of cost for the users, and they respond to people's need to have their day in court—without getting stuck with formalistic and lengthy court proceedings. The Lagos centers have so far reviewed more than 17,000 cases, resolving 15,950 of them amicably. Parties were advised to seek redress in court in only 332 cases.

Up to 25-30% of all commercial cases are resolved during the first 5 months of the proceedings, and average court delays are much reduced. Further improvements in efficiency are expected.

**Fewer cases go to court.** The citizens mediation centers in Lagos have handled 17,000 cases so far, many of which would normally have ended up in court. A large number of cases are now filed at the mediation centers because they are resolved faster, at a lower cost. In 2004, inspired by the enormous success of the centers in Lagos, all 35 state attorneys general decided to establish similar centers. In 12 Nigerian states, mediation centers all already in operation.

**Fewer cases stay in court.** During pretrial conferences, judges meet with the parties informally and explain to each the strengths and weaknesses of the case. They tell the parties what the outcome of the case is likely to be if the case were to go to trial. At the end of the meeting, the parties decide either to settle the case or go to trial. The judge drafts a pretrial conference report, describing the history of the case, the issues the parties are disputing, and the outcome of the pretrial conference. If the parties decide the case should still go to trial, the case is allocated to another judge, to avoid conflicts of interest between the judge acting as mediator and the judge acting as adjudicator.

Because of the mandatory pretrial conferences, up to 30% of all commercial cases are now disposed within the first 5 months of filing. Before the new rules were in place, all cases, once filed, stayed in court until a final decision was reached. To insure the continued success of pretrial conferences judges must be trained in their new role as mediators.

**Average court delays reduced.** For commercial cases the average time to reach a decision after filing a case dropped by 38%, from 730 days to 457. That moved Nigeria from 105th to 66th position in the Doing Business rankings for contract enforcement. In cases where defendants do not persuade the judge that they have a reasonable defense, summary judgments can be given in about 8 months.

## Reform is like repairing a car with the engine running

Nearly 85% of reforms take place in the first 15 months of a new government. Recently elected governments try to push reforms through at the start of their term, as Lagos did.

It did not take years of careful strategizing to build new courtrooms and repair existing ones. Less than a year after Osinbajo was appointed as attorney general of Lagos, 26 judges were appointed, specialized divisions set up, and judges' salaries increased.

Many judicial reforms fail because they address symptoms, not the problem's roots. To be effective, judicial reform must address all relevant issues at once, including: attracting and retaining the right people at the bench, disciplining lawyers who engage in delay tactics, establishing modern court rules, limiting the number of cases that go to court, limiting the number of inactive cases that stay in court for years, automating court procedures and measuring judicial performance.

Lagos did not only modernized its court rules, dismissed corrupt judges, and introduced alternative dispute resolution. It started a fight on all fronts, without allowing the challenges to affect its determination to provide a fair and efficient justice system, with access to justice for all.

**WHAT GETS MEASURED, GETS DONE.** Measuring performance enhances performance. This applies to all, including judges. If lazy judges are not disciplined and hard working judges are not compensated or promoted, performance flags.

The National Judicial Council monitors judicial performance at the federal level. In May 2006 officers from the Council traveled to the 36 Nigerian states to announce its ratings of individual judges. Those who scored poorly were invited to provide an explanation. Although the performance evaluation system is still developing and often criticized, judges now know they are being monitored by an institution with disciplinary power. This in itself has been useful: the poorest performers have already left the bench.

Measuring performance is useful at all levels, including the lowest: all support staff in the Lagos High Court must now submit weekly progress reports on the number of cases they enter in the court automation system. After Justice Abisoye Ayo collects the progress reports, she distributes them to all judges for them to see which staff members are performing well and which appear to be busy only when the judge is around. Healthy competition can do wonders.

**ADJUST FOREIGN MODELS TO LOCAL NEEDS.** Reformers often look abroad for inspiration. The citizens mediation centers were copied from the U.S. model, successful in large cities like New York. They do well because they are free and their procedures are simple.

But highly complex features from courts in developed countries cannot be easily transferred to developing countries. The committee in charge of the new Lagos High Court rules rejected the U.K. multiple case-track system because it was too advanced for Lagos.

**IMPLEMENTING REFORMS—AVOIDING ONE STEP FORWARD, TWO STEPS BACK.** Judicial reform needs constant fine-tuning. In Lagos the next challenges are establishing separate commercial courts with tailor-made rules for commercial cases and reducing the long delays before the appeals courts. Progress in the High Court risks being lost if reforms are not extended to the appeals court.

Initial positive results can disappear quickly, and disillusion over failed reforms can lead to questioning whether further reforms are worth the investment. To avoid the risk of going 1 step forward, 2 steps back, reforms must be implemented at all levels and their effects measured consistently.

That is why Lagos is now turning to its appeals courts. Of all cases pending before the appeals courts, 80% are against interlocutory orders from the High Court. Such orders deal with procedural issues, such as whether or not the court has jurisdiction to decide the case or whether the time limits to file have passed. Although High Court judges may continue to deal with cases while an interlocutory order is being appealed, some cases are suspended while waiting for the appeals court's decision. This is an important reason why the disposal time before the High Court is not faster and cases keep accumulating. Expanding the reforms and changing the appeals court rules can ensure progress continues.

# Faster, more orderly exit

Justin Yap

Winding up a failed Serbian enterprise could take 10 years or more. The entire bankruptcy process was susceptible to corruption by bankruptcy administrators and judges—including an infamous group known as the "bankruptcy mafia." After aggressive reforms, the average duration is now less than 3 years, and the procedure itself enjoys greater transparency and professionalism.

The new government that took power in January 2001, led by reformist Prime Minister Zoran Đinđić, faced a daunting task. Since the breakup of Yugoslavia in 1991-92, Serbia had become embroiled in one regional military conflict after another. These conflicts ravaged an economy already weakened by general government mismanagement. By 2000 Serbia's gross domestic product (GDP) was half that of 1989, public debt was 130% of GDP, and inflation hit 113%. Between 1994 and 2000 the Yugoslav dinar lost 97% of its value.

The Đinđić government made the privatization of state-owned enterprises a cornerstone of its liberalization program. In January 2001 Minister of Economy Aleksandar Vlahović announced that "4 years from now socially owned capital will be completely eliminated"; in June, Parliament passed a privatization law. But it soon became clear that more than 50 years of state planning and neglect had left a legacy that no privatization law alone could fix.

A World Bank report observed that a "functioning bankruptcy law is required in Serbia to provide an efficient alternative to the methods of privatization of social and state capital set out in the Privatization Law." The Ministry of Economy estimated that 3,000 enterprises were irretrievably inefficient and impossible to privatize through regular auctions and tenders. They would first have to be restructured and then privatized in bankruptcy proceedings. Bankruptcy reform in Serbia was thus closely linked to privatization.

The law then in effect—on forced settlement, bankruptcy, and liquidation—was not adequate. Courts applied it unevenly, opting in many cases for an unofficial and ad hoc "working bankruptcy" that prolonged the existence of uneconomical enterprises to prevent job losses. The law also failed to properly define the roles and responsibilities of bankruptcy administrators and creditors, and it contained no provision for reorganizing viable companies.

## Drafting and passing the new law

Vlahović, whose vision and support of the reform process were crucial in launching the bankruptcy reform, decided to push forward with plans to privatize Serbia's state and socially owned enterprises and introduce, in tandem, a new bankruptcy law at the republic level. He ordered a new law drafted in December 2001, delegating the task to an initial working group that included several commercial court judges, lawyers and law professors.

FIGURE 1
**How Serbia reformed bankruptcy law**

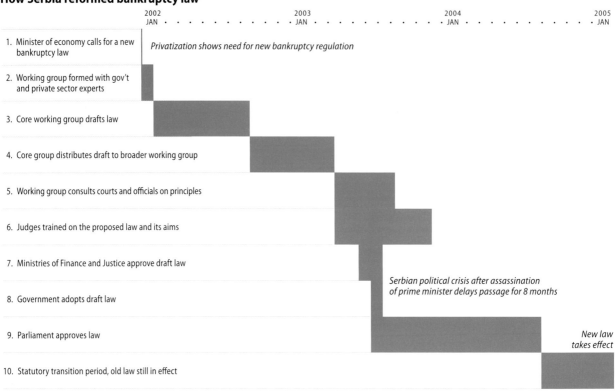

Source: *Doing Business* database.

Progress on the new law was relatively slow until 2003, when donor pressure and the need to fit the law into the Serbian parliament's schedule led Vlahović and Deputy Minister Mirko Čvetković to demand an accelerated timeframe. At his request, a group of 4 Serbian and several foreign experts from the World Bank and U.S. Agency for International Development (USAID) produced a first draft within the time demanded.

The core group submitted the draft for public consultation with various Serbian legal authorities, including judges of the commercial courts, the high commercial courts, and the Supreme Court of Serbia, as well as chambers of commerce, attorneys, and law professors. In addition, the chambers of commerce organized forums and roundtables to promote and discuss the draft law.

The Ministry of Economy distributed the draft to the Ministries of Finance, Justice, and Labor (as well as the major trade unions) for review and comment. After the Ministry of Economy reviewed the comments and finalized the draft text, the government of Serbia approved the draft on 5 June 2003. The draft was then handed over to a legislative panel to polish the text and prepare it for reading by Parliament.

Three months earlier, however, the assassination of Prime Minister Đinđić had plunged Serbia into a political crisis that now stalled the law's passage. A further setback: the December 2003 elections brought to power a government that had no interest in the proposed law and that withdrew the bill from Parliament. Only in March 2004 did the government pick up the draft again. In July 2004, Parliament approved a version of the draft revised slightly to include the UNCITRAL Model Provisions on Cross-Border Insolvency. The Law on Bankruptcy Proceedings entered into force on 2 August 2004 and took effect on 2 February 2005.

## Training administrators and judges

Training the administrators and judges was important in implementing the new law, which could work only if the parties with a direct hand in bankruptcy proceedings were familiar with the law. Serbia enlisted USAID and Germany's Gesellschaft für Technische Zusammenarbeit (GTZ) to put together training programs.

ADMINISTRATORS—VALUATIONS IN 22 MINUTES! USAID organized 6 seminars to train administrators. "The seminars focused on practical training," explains Milo Stevanović, the USAID consultant who assisted the committee in drafting the law. For example, the seminars tried to educate administrators on how to work within the new law's strict time limits. "Administrators thought it was impossible to perform a valuation in 30 days—they thought that 1 person would have to count every nut and bolt in the factory," Stevanović continues. "We brought in 1 professional trustee and asked him to give a valuation of the hotel where the conference was taking place. He came up with a valuation in 22 minutes—everyone was startled." Other seminars emphasized other practical issues, from demonstrating how many creditors' claims an administrator can evaluate in 1 hour, to how to conduct asset sales.

JUDGES—OBSERVING PROCEEDINGS FIRSTHAND IN LOS ANGELES. Soon after the release of the first draft, Serbian members of the original drafting group joined U.S. and German experts in touring the country's commercial courts to see the proposed changes.

USAID also sponsored 2 conferences for Serbian judges to discuss issues that arose in their practice, the first in Vršac, a town in the Vojvodina region near the Romanian border, and the second at Lepenski Vir, a significant archeological site in eastern Serbia. The new law met considerable resistance and skepticism at the Vršac conference, but the judges warmed to the law somewhat at Lepenski Vir, as they gradually became familiar with the reforms.

Some commercial court judges also had the opportunity to observe firsthand the workings of bankruptcy courts overseas. USAID consultant Stevanović led 3 groups of 8 commercial court judges on 1- or 2-week study tours to Los Angeles, to observe the U.S. Bankruptcy Court for the Central District of California in action. The judges saw how U.S. judges relied on attorneys to draft orders, used automation, and ran their back offices.

According to Stevanović, it was an "eye opener" for the judges to see the operational nuances of a court that works quickly, effectively, and efficiently: "One judge said she had thought the reforms were moving much too quickly, but once she saw how things worked in Los Angeles, she said she realized that 'we were incredibly behind and had to move much faster.' Another judge reported that, if he had had the clarity of what he saw in Los Angeles, he would never have opposed the changes in the law in the first place." In Stevanović's opinion, the study tours benefited the implementers of the reform as much as they benefited the judges: "For every dime we spent on [the tours], we saved time and effort on overcoming resistance from the judges. They were welcoming [the new law] instead of fighting it." Stevanović said that the study tours also bolstered USAID's credibility as reformers, as judges could "feel and taste and smell" for themselves that what they were being told was not just dry theory, but could be applied in their practice.

Training for judges did not end after Parliament passed the law. Beginning in June 2004 GTZ organized six 2-day seminars for Commercial Court judges, led by Judge Rudolf Voss, an experienced insolvency practitioner from Munich.

In 2006 GTZ organized 4 roundtables attended by 15–20 commercial court judges and representatives of the Privatization Agency and the Bankruptcy Supervision Agency. The roundtables allowed participants to discuss issues in implementing the new law, especially procedures involving socially owned enterprises. Based on the judges' own evaluations, the sessions were a "comprehensive success." Miloš Baltić, coordinator for GTZ, observes, "Although both sides were reluctant to open the dialogue at first, after the first half hour, it was difficult to get them to stop talking."

## Eliminating delays

Lawyers, administrators, judges on the High Commercial Court, and officials in the Bankruptcy Supervision Agency, while voicing some reservations, declared themselves satisfied with the reform. One attorney noted that bankruptcy procedures now move much faster and that there is no room for delays and uncertainties. Other improvements include the enhancement of the role of creditors and the more stringent qualifications required of bankruptcy administrators. According to Jay Allen, insolvency counsel at the European Bank for Reconstruction and

Development (ERBD), the reform "leads the way in the region." Meanwhile, the World Bank commended the law as being "designed to minimize the impact of existing institutional deficiencies in the judiciary and the trustee community."

The Bankruptcy Supervision Agency is one of the real innovations of Serbia's bankruptcy law, especially in the Balkans and continental Europe. An agency within the Ministry of Economy, it was created to regulate the bankruptcy administrator profession. Robert Gourley, one of the architects of the reform, says that his experience with the Canadian licensing system led him to promote a similar system in Serbia. The code of ethics and professional standards for bankruptcy administrators was another major step. So far 412 individuals have passed the licensing exam for bankruptcy administrators, 339 are licensed by the agency, and 237 are involved in bankruptcy cases.

**The law measurably improved all the major areas it was intended to address**

STRICT DEADLINES. The reforms set clear timeframes for completing particular parts of the bankruptcy procedure. The average time for a company to go through bankruptcy has fallen from 7.3 years to only 2.7. This shorter duration has also reduced the cost of bankruptcy and enhanced recovery for creditors. All wage, rent, and utility expenses incurred by the distressed company after the start of proceedings are considered bankruptcy costs and have priority over the claims of unsecured creditors.

CLEARLY DEFINED ROLES OF BANKRUPTCY ADMINISTRATORS. The new law requires the bankruptcy administrator to consult with creditors on most important decisions. For example, the bankruptcy administrator must now obtain creditors' written consent before selling any assets, taking a loan, or granting a lien.

REDUCED CORRUPTION. Only time will tell whether the new law eliminates corruption. But the law puts in place several mechanisms that discourage collusion: the licensing of bankruptcy administrators; the separation of powers among judges, administrators, and creditors; and creditors' greater ability to influence and determine outcomes. The new law also requires creditors' written consent for assets to be sold through direct negotiations with a private buyer.

PRIORITY RANKINGS TO CREDITORS' BENEFIT. Secured creditors now enjoy a "super-secured" position that stands above and apart from the priority rankings granted to other categories of creditors and claims: (1) bankruptcy costs, including post-bankruptcy wages, rent and utilities; (2) pre-bankruptcy wages up to 1 year, and unpaid social security and health contributions for up to 2 years, before the opening of the bankruptcy proceedings; (3) tax claims up to 3 months before the opening of the case; (4) all other creditors. The time requirements reduce the claims related to bankruptcy costs and pre-bankruptcy wages, benefiting unsecured creditors.

HIGHER QUALIFICATIONS FOR BANKRUPTCY ADMINISTRATORS. Although many of the administrators who passed licensing exams were also administrators under the old system, Jovan Jovanović, director of the Bankruptcy Supervision Agency, reports that the licensing requirements have had a positive effect on administrators' sense of professionalism. The pass rate was only about 20–25% for the first exams, but 50% for the last exam. Jovanović said that this increase was due to administrators "taking their jobs more seriously."

## Buy-in is crucial

Obtaining the buy-in of the various stakeholders was crucial to the reform's success, but also an area with lessons for future reforms in Serbia and elsewhere. Meetings with union representatives to vet the law allowed the unions to feel that they could have their say. And in the end the unions came out for the law because they received a (capped) wage priority claim that nonetheless ranked near the top.

Not all stakeholders gave their unequivocal buy-in. Despite the apparent success of the training for judges, perceptions of judges' acceptance of the new law are mixed. Gourley, one of the key people behind the reform, explained that, by altering the balance of power between judges and creditors, the new law "undermined not only [judges'] independence but also their freedom of action." That, of course, was precisely the point. As a result, the law was never widely accepted among all judges, and today a segment of the judiciary consists either of passive cooperators or judges who are actively trying to undermine the law.

One unique outcome of Serbia's bankruptcy reform is the emergence of an ad hoc committee that groups representatives from the Privatization Agency, USAID, and GTZ, as well as 2 supreme court judges, 2 high commercial court judges, and 6 commercial court judges. At its biweekly meetings, 20–25 people discuss issues in the day-to-day practice and implementation of the bankruptcy law. The issues raised—typically 5 or 6 per meeting—are tracked and recorded on a grid. The meetings help prevent misunderstanding and make it easier to get stakeholders' buy-in, since interested parties can voice their concerns and respond to real-life issues that crop up in implementing the law.

**New bankruptcy supervisory agency—a great success, but...**

The Bankruptcy Supervisory Agency is generally recognized as one of the great successes of the reform. But there is disagreement over whether it has assumed the full mantle of duties it was intended to take on. It has been very successful in training administrators, instituting professional standards, conducting examinations, and issuing licenses. But it has not yet assumed its intended supervisory and—especially—disciplinary functions, stymied by a nonbinding supreme court opinion limiting its regulatory functions.

One observer, to remain anonymous, says, "The agency was told, 'You're the regulator' and the response was 'What's a regulator? You can't expect someone to make fire if they haven't seen fire before.'" That makes it easy for the agency to stray out of areas it was supposed to regulate into areas where it was not.

Overall, however, Serbia's experience of bankruptcy reform appears to be an example of a generally successful reform that continues to inspire efforts to further improve the country's bankruptcy law.

# Acknowledgments

The case studies were sponsored by the *Doing Business* project and United States Agency for International Development.

Amy Allen, Tom Jersild (independent consultant), Jim McNicholas (independent consultant), Kiril Minoski, James Newton, Farah Sheriff, Zoran Skopljak participated in preparation of the case studies by Booz Allen Hamilton Inc. on behalf of USAID.

Doug Balko, Caroline Brearley, Jelena Bulatovic, Wade Channell, Irina Gordeladze, David Gosney, Peter Lampesis, Margareta Lipkovska, Mario Martinez, Steven Ndele, Cory O'Hara, Mark Pickett, Maja Piscevic, Amy Cogan Wares, Lisa Whitley of USAID provided comments and review.

The case studies were edited by Bruce Ross-Larson and designed and produced by Gerry Quinn.

The project was made possible by the generous contribution of more than 100 public officials, lawyers and business people, including:

## EGYPT

Ashraf Al Arabi
*DEPUTY MINISTER FOR TAX POLICY*

Amr ELmonayer
*SENIOR ASSISTANT TO DEPUTY MINISTER OF FINANCE*

Mohamed Fahim
*PRICEWATERHOUSECOOPERS, CAIRO*

Sherif Mansour
*PRICEWATERHOUSECOOPERS, CAIRO*

Geerten Michielse
*ECONOMIST, INTERNATIONAL MONETARY FUND*

Terrence Murdoch
*USAID, CAIRO*

Victor Thuronyi
*INTERNATIONAL MONETARY FUND*

## EL SALVADOR

Mayra de Morán
*DIRECTOR OF THE COMMISSION FOR THE STUDY OF REFORMS TO THE COMMERCIAL CODE*

Felix Safie
*DIRECTOR, THE NATIONAL CENTRAL REGISTRY*

Manuel del Valle
*DIRECTOR OF THE COMMERCIAL REGISTRY (JUNE 2003)*

Eduardo Zablah-Touche
*HEAD OF THE TECHNICAL SECRETARIAT OF THE PRESIDENCY*

## GEORGIA

David Abuladze, Chairperson
*UNION OF ARCHITECTS OF GEORGIA*

Zaza Bibilashvili
*PARTNER, BGI LEGAL ADVISORY SERVICES, TBILISI*

Temur Bolotashvili
*TEAM LEADER ON CONSTRUCTION TECHNICAL STANDARDS, USAID*

Vazha Chopikashvili
*FORMER HEAD OF REGISTRATION OFFICE, NATIONAL AGENCY OF THE PUBLIC REGISTRY; DIRECTOR OF IPRC*

Amy Denman
*EXECUTIVE DIRECTOR, AMERICAN CHAMBER OF COMMERCE IN GEORGIA*

Teimuraz Diasamidze
*DIRECTOR, ARCHSTUDIO CONSTRUCTION COMPANY*

Jaba Ebanoidze
*BOARD MEMBER OF ASSOCIATION FOR THE PROTECTION OF LAND OWNERS' RIGHTS*

Giorgi Gelovani
*INTERNATIONAL FINANCE CORPORATION, TBILISI*

David Georgadze
*FORMER HEAD OF REGISTRATION OFFICE, NATIONAL AGENCY OF THE PUBLIC REGISTRY; ASSOCIATION FOR THE PROTECTION OF LAND OWNERS' RIGHTS*

Giorgi Isakadze
*EXECUTIVE DIRECTOR, FEDERATION OF GEORGIAN BUSINESSES*

Acknowledgments

Natia Jokhadze
OFFICIAL, MINISTRY OF ECONOMY'S DEPARTMENT OF URBAN-IZATION AND CONSTRUCTION

Gia Kakauridze
DEPUTY HEAD OF CONSTRUCTION AND URBANIZATION DEPARTMENT OF MINISTRY OF ECONOMY

Gia Kurtskalia
DIRECTOR, MAGI STYLE CONSTRUCTION FIRM, TBILISI

Vakhtang Lejava
DEPUTY MINISTER, STATE MINISTRY FOR REFORM COORDINATION

Joseph Salukvadze
CHAIR, TBILISI STATE UNIVERSITY

Dave Sharp
DIRECTOR OF INTERNATIONAL CONSULTANCY, REGISTERS OF SCOTLAND EXECUTIVE AGENCY

Lela Shatirishvili
MANAGER, TBILISI TITLE COMPANY

George Tsagareli
PROJECT MANAGER, SILKROAD GEORGIA

Tato Urjumelashvili
COMMERCIAL LAW TEAM LEADER, USAID, TBILISI

## MACEDONIA, FYR

Mile Boskov
PRESIDENT OF THE CONFEDERATION OF THE EMPLOYERS OF THE REPUBLIC OF MACEDONIA

Marko Culev
PART-TIME EMPLOYEE AT FX3X

Milivoje Dzordevic
MANAGER AND OWNER OF FX3X

Nikola Eftimov
FEDERATION OF TRADE UNIONS OF MACEDONIA (SSM)

Dragan Jovanovski
HEAD OF THE LEGAL DEPARTMENT OF A LABOR UNION

Valentino Konstantinovski
MANAGER AND OWNER OF ETAPA PROJECT

Arvo Kuddo
SENIOR LABOR ECONOMIST, WORLD BANK

Slagjan Mihajlovski
MANAGER AND OWNER OF INFINITE SOLULTIONS

Evgenij Najdov
ECONOMIST, WORLD BANK, SKOPJE

Aco Spasevski
MACEDONIAN CHAMBER OF COMMERCE

Darko Velkov
MANAGER OF VRABOTUVANJE.COM (EMPLOYMENT.COM) AND OWNER WITH VRABOTUVANJE LEASING

## MEXICO

Jorge Familiar Calderón
EXECUTIVE DIRECTOR, WORLD BANK

José Antonio González Anaya
DIRECTOR GENERAL, SECURITIES & INSURANCE, MINISTRY OF FINANCE

Eugenia González Rivas
JUNIOR PARTNER, GOODRICH, RIQUELME Y ASOCIADOS

Yves Hayaux - du -Tilly Laborde
PARTNER, JAUREGUÍ, NAVARRETE Y NADER S.C.

Jorge Sánchez
JUNIOR PARTNER, GOODRICH, RIQUELME Y ASOCIADOS

## NIGERIA

Habeeb Adewale Olumuyiwa Abiru
JUDGE IN THE LAND DIVISION AT THE LAGOS HIGH COURT

Augustine Adetula Ade-Alabi
CHIEF JUDGE OF LAGOS STATE

Adolphous Akwumakwuhie
ASSOCIATE ATTORNEY AT ALUKE & OYEBODE

Joanna Kata Blackman
CONSULTANT, WORLD BANK

Abisoye Esther Ayo
JUDGE IN THE COMMERCIAL DIVISION AT THE LAGOS HIGH COURT IN CHARGE OF THE CAIS PROJECT

Anse Agu Ezetah
PARTNER AT CHIEF LAW AGU EZETAH & CO.

Tunde Fagbohunlu
ATTORNEY AT ALUKO & OYEBODE, FORMER MEMBER ON THE COMMITTEE ESTABLISHING THE 2004 HIGH COURT RULES

Jean Paul Gauthier
CONSULTANT, WORLD BANK

Danladi Halilu
SECRETARY AT THE NATIONAL JUDICIAL COUNCIL

Ade Ipaye
SENIOR SPECIAL ASSISTANT (LEGAL MATTERS) TO THE GOVERNOR OF LAGOS STATE

O. Atinuke Ipaye
*Judge in the Commercial Division at the Lagos High Court*

Alh. Muktari A. Tambawel
*Deputy Director at the National Judicial Council*

Yemi Osinbajo
*Attorney General & Commissioner for Justice of Lagos State*

Emiola Oyefuga
*Senior State Program Officer, UK DFID Security, Justice and Growth Program Nigeria*

## PAKISTAN

Manzoor Ahmad
*Ambassador and Permanent Representative of Pakistan to the WTO*

## PANAMA

Germán Espinosa
*Business and Alliances Manager, Panamanian Credit Association*

Oscar Madeddu
*International Finance Corporation*

Luz Maria Salamina
*Executive Director, Panamanian Credit Association*

Nora Sheblelut
*Panamanian Credit Association*

## SERBIA

Jay Allen, Miloš Baltić, Nataša Cvetićanin, Predrag Dejanović
*Attorney at Law, Ninković Law Office*

Aleksandar Dmitrov
*Attorney at Law, Prica & Partners*

Nikola Đorđević
*Attorney at Law, Janković, Popović & Mitić*

Jelena Edelman
*Attorney at Law, Prica & Partners*

Jelena Gazivoda
*Attorney at Law, Janković, Popović & Mitić*

Robert Gourley
*Senior Private Sector Development Specialist, The World Bank, Advisor to the Privatization Agency of the Ministry of Economy*

Hugo Green
*Advisor to the Serbian Privatisation Agency Bankruptcy Unit and to Serbian Bankruptcy Supervision Agency*

Jovan Jovanović
*Director, Bankruptcy Supervision Agency of the Republic of Serbia*

Biljana Kozlovic
*Advisor, USAID-Serbian Enterprise Development Project*

Branka Kulić
*Deputy Director, Bankruptcy Supervision Agency of the Republic of Serbia*

Radomir Lazarević
*President, High Commercial Court of the Republic of Serbia*

Andreja Marusic
*Attorney at Law, Council for Regulatory reform and Chair of the Board of SBRA*

Mihajlo Prica
*Attorney at Law, Prica & Partners*

Maja Piscevic
*Senior Legal Advisor, Economics and Governance Office USAID/ US Embassy Belgrade*

Momir Radic
*Attorney at Law, Radic Law Office*

Dragana Stanojevic
*Deputy Chief of Party, USAID/Bankruptcy and Enforcement Strengthening Activity (BES)*

Milo Stevanović, Chief of Party
*Bankruptcy and Enforcement Strengthening, Commercial Court Administration Strengthening Activity, Booz Allen Hamilton*

Jelisaveta Vasilić
*former Justice, High Commercial Court of the Republic of Serbia*

Djordje Vukotic
*Attorney at Law, Council for Regulatory Reform*

Tanja Unguran
*Attorney at Law, CMS Reich-Rohrwig Hasche Sigle d.o.o.*